MICHI CHALLENGES HISTORY

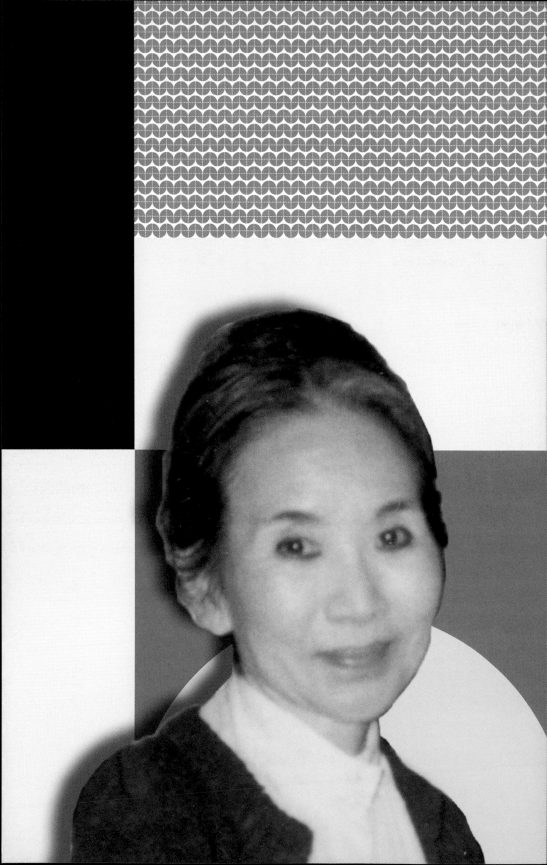

KEN MOCHIZUKI

MICHI CHALLENGES HISTORY

From Farm Girl to Costume
Designer to Relentless Seeker
of the Truth: The Life of
MICHI NISHIURA WEGLYN

Norton Young Readers

An Imprint of W. W. Norton & Company
Celebrating a Century of Independent Publishing

For information about permission to reproduce selections from this book, write to
Permissions, W. W. Norton & Company, Inc., 500 Fifth Avenue, New York, NY 10110

For information about special discounts for bulk purchases, please contact
W. W. Norton Special Sales at specialsales@wwnorton.com or 800-233-4830

Manufacturing by Versa Press, Inc.
Book design by Hana Anouk Nakamura
Production managers: Anna Oler & Beth Steidle

Library of Congress Cataloging-in-Publication Data

Names: Mochizuki, Ken, 1954– author.
Title: Michi challenges history : from farm girl to costume designer to relentless seeker of
the truth: the life of Michi Nishiura Weglyn / Ken Mochizuki.
Description: First edition. | New York, NY : Norton Young Readers, An Imprint of W. W. Norton
& Company, [2023] | Includes bibliographical references and index. | Audience: Ages: 13–18
Identifiers: LCCN 2022009733 | ISBN 9781324015888 (cloth) | ISBN 9781324015895 (epub)
Subjects: LCSH: Weglyn, Michi Nishiura, 1926–1999—Juvenile literature. | Japanese
American women—Biography—Juvenile literature. | Costume designers—United States—
Biography—Juvenile literature. | Japanese Americans—Forced removal and internment,
1942–1945—Juvenile literature. | Japanese Americans—Reparations—Juvenile literature.
Classification: LCC E184.J3 M585 2022 | DDC 973/.04956092 [B]—dc23/eng/20220606
LC record available at https://lccn.loc.gov/2022009733

W. W. Norton & Company, Inc., 500 Fifth Avenue, New York, N.Y. 10110
www.wwnorton.com

W. W. Norton & Company Ltd., 15 Carlisle Street, London W1D 3BS

0 9 8 7 6 5 4 3 2 1

That she become more well known:
Michi Nishiura Weglyn,
fighter for the "forgotten ones"

CONTENTS

Issei

The first generation of Japanese in the United States, immigrants who were prohibited until 1952 from becoming U.S. citizens.

Nisei

The second generation, children of the Issei, born in the United States and therefore U.S. citizens.

Kibei

Nisei born in the United States, sent to Japan to be educated there, then returned to America.

Sansei

The third generation, children of the Nisei, grandchildren of the Issei.

chapter 1

Until we extend the circle of our compassion
to all living things, man will not himself find peace.
—Michi Nishiura Weglyn,
quoting Dr. Albert Schweitzer

MICHIKO NISHIURA GREW UP ON A FARM
that went on for five hundred acres of forever. Her parents and relatives labored in the fields under the constant central California sun, growing cucumbers and tomatoes, apricots and cantaloupes. Young Michiko wandered among the horses and chickens, played with the cats and dogs, talked to the possum and parrot.

On rare occasions, chickens were born bald, without feathers. Did they have to live the rest of their lives that way? Michiko wondered. They needed help. She sketched her ideas on paper, then measured, cut, and sewed furry little sweaters for them. They didn't have to suffer because of the way they had been born.

Neither did the abandoned kittens left in gunnysacks on the side of the road by neighbors who knew Michiko and her sister Tomiko would take them in. Their mother, unable to afford to feed any more animals, tried to get rid of them as soon as they were found. Michiko and Tomiko tried to add them to their menagerie before their mother returned from the fields.

Michiko's family worked for the owner of all that land. They lived on the first floor of a grand but deteriorated house on a former estate where croquet had once been played among the fig and olive trees. The farmworkers whom her father supervised lived on the floors above. During harvest time, many more migrant workers rode in to live in the other structures still standing, like the barns and sheds, or pitched tents on what used to be the expansive and manicured front lawn.

Michiko knew that her parents wished she had been born a boy. Then they would have a son to grow up and continue operating the farm and carry on the family name. For the Japanese families, it was considered crucial for the firstborn to be a capable son. So Michiko went out and fed the chickens and horses before school, to show she was as good as any son. Driving the Ford truck, she brought workers out to the fields during the summer. At night as her family watered the crops, Michiko carried a kerosene lantern. Her job was to wait at the end of dry irrigation ditches and wave the lantern to signal to her father that the water reached where she stood.

Tomojiro Nishiura, Michiko's father, left Osaka, Japan, in 1916—one of those who joined the wave of immigration to America during the turn of the nineteenth century into the twentieth. Young men in search of a future left as Japan's sweeping industrialization, begun in the mid-1800s to match the major powers of the West, edged out the country's centuries-old reliance on agriculture, and heavy taxes levied by the government became a burden on farmers. Men hoping to escape the military draft also fueled the exodus from Japan, as did unemployed veterans of the 1904–05 Russo-Japanese War and World War I.

And then there were those young men who had no choice due to an unyielding Japanese cultural tradition of the time: the firstborn son in a family inherited everything—the family name, the house, the property, and the family business. All the boys other than the firstborn were left to determine their own destinies. Girls were expected to marry and become members of other families.

One way young Japanese women were able to leave Japan for America was by becoming a "picture bride." Based almost entirely on an exchange of photographs, an immigrant bachelor chose a wife and met her in person for the first time on the dock of an American port. The new couple married that day or the day after. That was the way Michiko's parents met: in 1922 Tomojiro Nishiura selected Misao Yuasa from Wakayama Prefecture, and married her.

Tomojiro and Misao, and members of Misao's family who also immigrated, farmed land in Brentwood, a small town midway between

Oakland and Stockton in California's San Joaquin Valley. However, they could never own the land they toiled on: American laws prohibited immigrants from Asia from acquiring and owning property.

Michiko was born in Stockton on November 29, 1926. Two years later, her younger sister Tomiko came along.

Michi's mother, Misao Nishiura, with Michi as a baby, sits for a studio portrait in 1926.

Tomojiro and Misao Nishiura "in their last formal photo prior to entering camp," Michi writes beneath the photo, taken about 1940.

As a girl, and one of Japanese descent, Michiko had to know her place, her parents taught her. What others thought of her was what she should be most concerned about. According to Japanese cultural etiquette, she had to practice self-restraint, place the needs and desires of others ahead of her own, and not call attention to herself. If she failed to do so, then she must endure *haji*—shame, dishonor to the family name. Growing up, Michiko became fascinated by costumes and clothing design, by Ziegfeld Follies movies and Hollywood musical extravaganzas—but no use dreaming of becoming an actress, Michiko's mother advised.

Duty to country comes first, her parents also instilled in her, and their country was America, the one that allowed them to live and work as they wished—even though U.S. law ruled that Asian immigrants could not become American citizens. She must not offend, especially not her white peers and "superiors." The president of the United States was to be held in the highest of esteem, similar to how the emperor was back in Japan.

At school, Michiko made friends with those who looked and were more like her—Filipino and Mexican American students whose parents were also farmworkers. She wanted others to have only good impressions about her. At Excelsior School and Liberty Union High School in Brentwood, she was recognized for being an exceptional student and received a citizenship award from the American Legion. She placed first in a Rotary Club essay contest about the U.S. Constitution.

"Michiko Nishiura of Excelsior School is selected for this award because she is found to possess, among others, those high qualities of character—Courage, Character, Service, Companionship and Scholarship which are necessary to the preservation and protection of the fundamental institutions of our government and the advancement of society," stated the American Legion Certificate of School Award.

Together with being the best student she could be, Michiko knew to stay quiet, to know her place; knew that she, of Japanese descent and among others whose parents were not sharecroppers like hers, would never be recognized as the smartest or most popular student.

The American Legion Certificate
of
School Award

This certifies that   Michiko Nishiura

of   Excelsior   School,

is selected for this award because she is found to possess,
among others, those high qualities of character-Courage,
Character, Service, Companionship and Scholarship
which are necessary to the preservation and protection of
the fundamental institutions of our government and the
advancement of society.

This award is made by Roy Frerichs
Post No. 202, The Department of California
The American Legion on June 10   1940

ATTEST:

_____   _____
POST ADJUTANT   POST COMMANDER

*This American Legion certificate is awarded to
Michi while a student at Excelsior School, 1940.*

chapter 2

This, under the circumstances, was the only way to prove our loyalty to a country which we loved. . . . In an inexplicable spirit of atonement and with great sadness, we went with our parents to concentration camps.

—Michi Nishiura Weglyn

DURING THE 1920S, ON THE OTHER SIDE of the world, Japan's military took control of the country. Needing natural resources to feed its war machine, it later conquered territory in China, Southeast Asia, the Pacific Islands. The United States, opposed to Japan's brutal and relentless aggression, placed embargoes that prevented the delivery of necessary material to Japan, including oil and iron. On December 7, 1941, Japan attacked the U.S. naval fleet stationed at Pearl Harbor, Hawaii.

Michiko knew none of this, only what she and her family heard as they sat around the kitchen table and listened to the radio that Sunday. As they first heard of that attack by Japanese aircraft on the

American ships and grounded planes, Michiko read the looks on her parents' faces. It was as if they were the ones who had been snuck up on and attacked. How could the country they came from do such a thing to the country that was their new home?

Michiko worried about the next day at school. Would she and her fellow Japanese American students, who knew no country but America, be harassed or assaulted by other students because they had Japanese faces and names? Should she even go to school?

Luckily, her teacher, who knew the difference between the Japanese in America and the actions of the country of Japan, pronounced that the attack was not the fault of their fellow students and they were not to be blamed.

But Michiko listened to the worried conversations at home among her parents and relatives. Would other Americans see that difference, that the Japanese in America like them had nothing to do with Japan's attack on the United States? Would they be considered more Japanese than American, and loyal to Japan? Since they were prevented from becoming citizens of America, they were still citizens of Japan. Would they be treated as such? Should they be apologizing, seeking atonement from other Americans for what their mother country had done, as some immigrants from Japan were then doing? Then perhaps nothing bad might happen to them.

Michiko heard from other Japanese American students at her school and from her parents and relatives that FBI agents and local police were arresting influential local Japanese leaders who they claimed could be threats to the United States: the community club president, the minister of the Buddhist church, the principal at the Japanese language school, the judo and kendo instructors, the Japanese-language-newspaper publisher, those who had more contact with the country of Japan than others. Who would be next?

The less connection to the country of Japan, the better. Michiko and Tomiko awoke at night to noises of rustling, ripping, and clanking. They looked out to see fires off in the middle of the fields. Adult family members were burning and burying objects that connected them to Japan, and especially to its military past: painted portraits, family photographs, books and letters written in Japanese, samurai swords.

But as news kept coming of the Japanese military achieving swift victories in the Pacific, the Japanese in America were hated even more. Was an invasion of the U.S. mainland next? American politicians and the press fueled the fear: Who among the Japanese living on the West Coast could be spies, saboteurs, would assist Japan's military when the invasion came? There was no time to find out—move them all out! President Roosevelt agreed, issuing Executive Order 9066 on February 19, 1942. It authorized the secretary of war to designate "military areas" and remove all persons without permission to remain.

Orders from the U.S. government were posted on telephone poles, lampposts, walls: all of Japanese descent, including those born in America—American citizens like Michiko—had to leave the western halves of the Pacific Coast states and a southern section of Arizona. The Nishiura family then had less than two weeks to pack before they

"Evacuation Orders" are posted in San Francisco, April 1942.

were to report to a designated location. And they could take with them only what they could carry. That it was true was brought home when Michiko's father returned from the government office with tags identifying the Nishiura family as a number, to be attached to themselves and their luggage. The date when the family was to be taken away was also there: May 2. No one knew where they were going, or for how long.

Michiko knew what was clawing through the minds of her parents. Since the Nishiuras could only live and work on the land and not own it, the farm would never be theirs to return to once they left. Others would take their place and live in their home. And Michiko worried about what would happen to all the farm animals. No pets were allowed where they were going.

*Families board buses in Byron, California, bound
for the Turlock Assembly Center, May 2, 1942.*

Her mother and father faced an agonizing dilemma: Sell everything that the family couldn't store or take with them? Or abandon it? Better to make some money than nothing, but Michiko's parents then had to deal with strangers swooping through to buy at bargain prices what the Nishiuras and other Japanese owned. The car, trucks, Michiko and Tomiko's bicycles disappeared. With so little time, Michiko's parents had no choice but to accept what they were offered. One stranger proposed to buy the chickens for a quarter apiece. Outraged by the insulting offer, Michiko's mother decided that the family would eat as many of the chickens as they could before they had to leave.

When the dreaded early morning came, a neighbor drove the

Nishiuras to the nearby town of Byron, the staging area for the Japanese from the surrounding farms. Michiko and Tomiko watched their lifelong feathered and furry friends disappear in the distance, and Michiko pondered what her family had done to have to face this. At Byron, the family joined others with suitcases and duffel bags— carrying with them what remained of a lifetime of hard work.

U.S. Army soldiers loaded them into Greyhound Lines buses and they were driven the sixty-five miles to the Stanislaus County fairgrounds at the town of Turlock, near Modesto. Barbed-wire fences, guard towers, and armed soldiers had turned the fairgrounds into the Turlock Assembly Center, one of fifteen fairgrounds and horse

Baggage is inspected as families arrive at the Turlock Assembly Center.

racetracks in California, Arizona, Oregon, and Washington converted into temporary detention centers for Japanese Americans.

The Nishiuras joined hundreds of others of Japanese descent, first formed into long lines to pass makeshift tables of plywood atop sawhorses to have their luggage inspected by civilian volunteers. Could some of the men searching for "contraband"—weapons of any kind, cameras, maps—have been members of the American Legion that, two years earlier, had given Michiko the American citizenship award?

Used to her wide-open farm, Michiko found herself crammed into a hastily built, tar-papered barrack, where her family was quartered all together in one room. They ate, showered, and used the latrine with all the others—never with any privacy. Soldiers conducted a head count at 9 p.m. and lights were turned out at 10 p.m. Michiko, her sister, and her parents slept on mattresses filled with straw.

While some adults worked jobs maintaining and running the Assembly Center, many only waited for what was to come next. Was Michiko thinking about what her life used to be like as a high school sophomore, as she listened to the discussions among the adults and older kids?

Some exploded in outrage at what had happened to them. What crimes had they committed? If this was for their own "protection" from dangerous citizens seeking revenge for the Pearl Harbor attack, as some in America claimed, why couldn't local law enforcement or the army have protected them where they lived? Why were the soldiers' guns and searchlights pointed into the camp at them, rather than outward at anyone who would do them harm?

Most sighed, resigned to their fate, and said they had to cooperate with the U.S. government to prove their loyalty to America and help with the country's war effort. There were even those who said they must have done something against their country, the United States, to end up where they were.

How long would they be there? As long as the war lasted? In June 1942, the Japanese navy suffered its first major defeat at the Battle of Midway. How much longer would the war go on?

chapter 3

I despise deserts and the sun.
For years, people didn't understand
why I walk in the shade.
—Michi Nishiura Weglyn

AFTER OVER THREE MONTHS AT TURLOCK,

Michiko and her family and the others at the Assembly Center were put on trains and transported over the jagged Sierra Nevada mountains and through the endless Mojave Desert. The journey lasted two days and nights and was prolonged as their train was forced to move over to the side, for hours at a time, to allow freight trains loaded with war matériel and supplies to pass through. The passengers were let out of the train during those times for relief from the constant sitting; armed U.S. Army soldiers stood guard—as if any of the Japanese Americans would try to escape.

Finally, they arrived at their destination: the Gila River War

Relocation Center on the Gila River Indian Reservation, about fifty miles south of Phoenix in southern Arizona. It was one of the ten main camps operated by the federal government, in Arizona, California, Colorado, Utah, Wyoming, Idaho, and Arkansas, to hold those of Japanese descent from the U.S. West Coast states and Alaska.

If Michiko had thought it was hot in central California, it was really hot here, with temperatures sometimes reaching over 120 degrees. She found herself with about thirteen thousand others in a much larger version of the Assembly Center in the middle of the desert, with saguaro cactus and sagebrush, rattlesnakes, and scorpions. White beaverboard barracks with red-shingled roofs were lined up as far as the eye could see.

The Gila River camp is built in the Arizona desert.

*On the back of this undated WRA photo of staff housing at Gila River,
Michi writes: "One of the glaring inequities between the administration and the
'administered' were the better built and furnished housing for Caucasians."*

The Gila River War Relocation Center was divided into two: Butte Camp sitting on its western half, Canal Camp to the east. About a dozen barracks formed a "block" with its own communal mess hall serving canned and often inedible food, latrines with toilets and showers without partitions, and a laundry room where clothes were scrubbed clean in tubs. The Nishiuras were assigned to the Butte Camp, where they lived with another family of four in a sixteen-by-twenty-foot room at Block 66, Barrack 12.

Like everyone else there, the Nishiuras found no relief from the heat. They tried sleeping outside at night, and Michiko sprinkled water around with a watering can to attempt to cool the room. There was always the powdery sandstorm dust—inside and outside. Wind-driven sand seeped through cracks in the walls and spaces around the windows. When Michiko stepped into the sand outside, it was like walking through flour, she thought. She carried an umbrella to shade herself from the searing sun and as a shield against the constant sandstorms. She and others wore water-soaked handkerchiefs over their noses and mouths.

The War Relocation Authority (WRA), the U.S. government agency operating the camps, tried to replicate some aspects of the everyday life its charges used to know. Adults could work jobs

Michi (right) with her sister, Tomi, are photographed by their barrack at the Gila River camp, about 1943.

maintaining and servicing the camps. Skilled professionals like doctors earned the top pay rate of $19 per month. Semiskilled workers such as farmers were paid $16, unskilled labor like kitchen help made $12.

Most of those at the Gila River camp were former farming families. Many of the farmers, including Michiko's father, worked the seven-thousand-acre farm connected to the camp, raising crops to feed those living there. Tomojiro became sick with valley fever, an illness particular to the U.S. Southwest, caused when a fungus beneath the soil is disturbed and its spores fly through the air and are inhaled by humans. For almost two years, including time confined to the camp hospital, he would suffer from flu-like symptoms accompanied by fatigue, aching joints, and red sores on his lower legs.

Jim Araki, president of the junior class, addresses an outdoor class at Butte High School, 1943.

For Michiko and Tomiko, school was held at classrooms in the barracks. Michiko attended Butte High School in Block 43 of the camp.

But here, unlike at high school back in Brentwood, the Japanese American students all dealt with the same things the same way: the heat and dust, the endless beans, mutton, and bland Vienna sausages, showering and using the latrines together. At the end of the day, they all returned to the same look-alike barrack rooms. Here, Michiko didn't have to constantly watch herself and know her place, for no one had it better than another. Although her mother tried to reinforce what Michiko had always been taught, that she was no more special than any other and must not call attention to herself, Michiko felt the need to express herself. She began to speak out. Why couldn't she be more of the American that she hadn't allowed herself to be before?

Michiko continued being the student she was before the war broke out, earning straight As and winning essay contests. But at Gila River, she also organized and became president of the Girl Scout troop—something she would have never dared to do back home at Brentwood. And besides, on the farm, she never had the time for anything but work and school. There in the camp, she led a troop of all Japanese American girls. To help pay for their uniforms, Michiko asked her mother to make sushi rolls to sell. The Japanese delicacy was a rare reprieve from camp food, and Michiko's troop made more money than they needed. When the U.S. government sponsored the sale of war bonds to help finance its war effort, she sold the most twenty-five-dollar war bonds to the Japanese American workers in the camp.

Girl Scouts parade at Gila River, 1943.
Michi was president of her troop.

In April 1943, Michiko was selected as one of the students to greet First Lady Eleanor Roosevelt when she arrived at Gila River on a surprise visit along with the War Relocation Authority director Dillon Myer.

What was she doing coming here, of all places? Michiko and her friends wondered. Little did they know that the First Lady was on a mission for her husband, to see for herself what one of these camps was really like. Americans outside the camps, including politicians, had begun to say that the Japanese Americans there were being "coddled," that they had it better than the rest of America, which was dealing with the rationing of consumer goods—everything from meat to sugar to gas—that needed to be diverted to the American troops overseas.

Nisei teenagers John Tachihara (left) and Kim Nagano speak to Eleanor Roosevelt, with Dillion Myer in the background, during their visit to Gila River in April 1943. Michi writes on the back of this photo, "And when our 'first lady' visited us, we knew we are not forgotten; when she came among us refusing guards, we knew she trusted us."

Mrs. Roosevelt and Mr. Myer toured Gila River and met with those in the camp. What did the First Lady think about what she saw and heard? What would she report back to her husband, the president?

Eleanor Roosevelt wrote an essay for *Collier's* magazine after her visit. In an earlier draft, she reported that she found no evidence of "coddling." "Neither in the stock-rooms, or on the tables did I notice any kind of extravagance," she wrote, and that those in the camp had it no better than any other American.

As for the reason why those of Japanese descent were in the

camps, Mrs. Roosevelt wrote that the "mistake" had been to allow America's immigrants to gather in self-contained communities that isolated them from the rest of America. Doing so contributed to their being seen as "different." Unfamiliarity with Japanese Americans had led to distrust and suspicion, which led to their removal from their homes and businesses on the U.S. West Coast.

Mrs. Roosevelt continued that "to undo a mistake is always harder than not to create one originally but we seldom have the foresight . . . to correct our past mistakes." Mrs. Roosevelt encouraged Americans who found those Japanese Americans resettled in their communities to "try to regard them as individuals" and "not to condemn them before they are given a fair chance to prove themselves in the community.

"'A Japanese is always a Japanese' is an easily accepted phrase and it has taken hold quite naturally on the West Coast because of fear, but it leads nowhere and solves nothing," Mrs. Roosevelt wrote. "A Japanese American may be no more Japanese than a German-American is German, or an Italian-American is Italian."

Eleanor Roosevelt concluded: "We retain the right to lead our individual lives as we please, but we can only do so if we grant to others the freedoms that we wish for ourselves."

Collier's magazine published a rewritten version of the First Lady's essay in October 1943. In this version, titled "A Challenge to American Sportsmanship," her visit to Gila River was never mentioned, nor was the accusation of "coddling" ever addressed.

chapter 4

At Gila, I was trying somehow

to regain my self-respect.

—Michi Nishiura Weglyn

AS A SENIOR IN 1944, MICHIKO SERVED as president of Butte High School's chapter of the Girls' League, an organization with chapters in schools throughout the state. The other high school at the Gila River camp, Canal, had its own chapter. That spring, Michiko proposed staging a Girls' League convention at the camp and inviting high school girls from outside. The Butte and Canal Girls' League chapters formed committees to plan the daylong event, to take place on a Saturday at Butte High School.

The Girls' League newspaper, the *Girls' League Gazette*, quoted Michiko: "We hope by means of this convention, to establish a firmer bond among the girls who attend in understanding and facing our problems together and in aiding each other in solving them."

*Michi lives at the Gila River camp from August 1942
to July 1944. Photo taken in 1943.*

On April 8, 1944, at 8:30 a.m., 513 female students converged at Butte. According to the *Gila News-Courier*, the camp newspaper, 200 were from Butte, 168 from Canal; other schools represented "were Chandler (25), North Phoenix (22), Phoenix Union (18), Scottsdale (15), Tempe (12), Coolidge (12), Peoria (10), Tolleson (10), Mesa (8) and the Phoenix Indian School (3)."

Michiko was among those delivering the opening welcome, which was followed by an "Exchange of Talent" at the camp's outdoor amphitheater and a sports competition including basketball, tennis, track events, and softball. The students ate the camp food

Michi (front, fourth from right), Girls' League president, is photographed with her cabinet. In the back row, center, is their faculty adviser, Jane Eckenstein. Photo taken in 1944.

during a lunch together at Butte High School's mess hall, followed by an extensive tour of the Gila River War Relocation Center. They then broke up into discussion groups. Topics included "The Basis of Popularity in High School," "My Parents and I," "Making a Future in America," "How We Can Help in the War Effort," and "Preparing for Marriages."

According to coverage in the *Gila News-Courier*: "Discussions were conducted in the afternoon with the unanimous conclusion that regardless of race, creed or color, nisei in the camp merit the title of American just as much as any other. They also agreed that although this convention could not have been attended by more, the representatives of the various schools will be able to go back

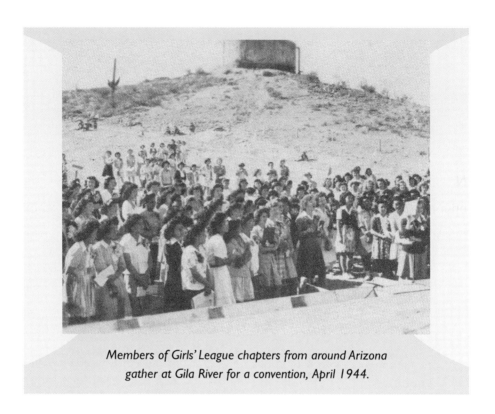

*Members of Girls' League chapters from around Arizona
gather at Gila River for a convention, April 1944.*

and tell others more about those in relocation centers. They felt
that the reason for racial prejudice and war was largely due to lack
of education, and this must be built upon as one of the greatest
foundations for the America in which they shall lead. During these
discussions many of the doubts in the minds of the visitors as to
relocation, combat teams, coddling, and such were made much
clearer."

Despite her fear that her mind would go blank in the middle of
a speech, Michiko was an accomplished public speaker. She was a

leader on Butte High's debate team. That year, she placed first in an oratory competition for contestants at the Butte Camp, speaking on the topic "How Evacuation Affected Me"—"evacuation" being the government term for the ouster of Japanese Americans from their homes and businesses. Reporting on the contest, the *Gila News-Courier* remarked: "With poise, excellent diction, and perfect enunciation, unusual in any American or Japanese American, youthful Michiko Nishiura related her reaction to evacuation to win the coveted first place gold trophy."

Around that same time, Michiko also took first place in the "pure declamation division" in the Declamation Contest sponsored by Butte High. She read a March 30, 1944, speech delivered by Missouri state representative O. K. Armstrong on the floor of the Missouri House of Representatives. Armstrong, a World War I U.S. Army veteran, spoke against a proposed legislative bill amendment that sought to remove a doctor of Japanese descent from practicing in the Missouri State Sanatorium. It concluded:

"There can be no world peace unless it be founded upon the principles of justice, mercy and understanding among all peoples. Let us then deny the implication that white Americans are the super race. Grateful as I am for my heritage, I cannot take credit for being born a white man. That was God's will. And if I were a Japanese, or the son of any other race, and could be born in this land of liberty, I would thank God that I am an American citizen.

"Let us lift our voices against any moves toward discrimination because of color or creed. If interracial bigotry and intolerance raise their ugly heads and lift their reeking banners in other lands, or even in other states of this Union, let Missouri remain forever a refuge to tolerance, a haven of good will toward men."

Michiko was recognized with the 1944 Butte High School Student Council Award "for having contributed the most outstanding piece of work during this year to the activities of Butte High School." As "the most outstanding girl of the '44 class," according to the *Gila News-Courier*, she also received her second American Legion Certificate of School Award for the same reasons she had received the honor four years earlier in 1940, in a different school under different conditions and circumstances: "those high qualities of Courage, Character, Service, Companionship and Scholarship which are necessary to the preservation and protection of the fundamental institutions of our government and the advancement of society."

᠁᠁᠁᠁᠁᠁᠁᠁᠁᠁᠁᠁᠁᠁᠁᠁᠁᠁᠁᠁᠁᠁᠁᠁᠁᠁

The camps continued operating, even though by mid-1944 Japan was losing the war and no longer posed a threat of attacking the United States. However, the previous year the War Relocation Authority had begun allowing Japanese Americans to leave the camps, provided that they sought work or attended schools away from the U.S. West Coast. An organization called the National Japanese American Student Relocation Council, a coalition composed of American

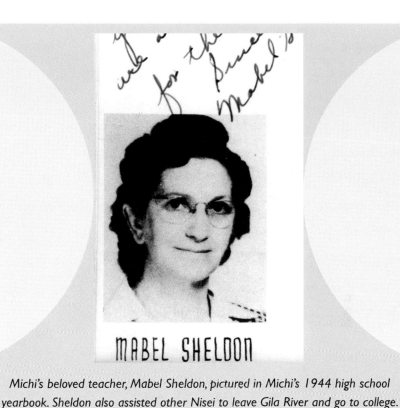

MABEL SHELDON

Michi's beloved teacher, Mabel Sheldon, pictured in Michi's 1944 high school yearbook. Sheldon also assisted other Nisei to leave Gila River and go to college.

religious organizations, including the Quakers, had been making arrangements for students like Michiko to attend college.

Michiko had caught the attention of her Butte High School English teacher, Mabel Sheldon. In Miss Sheldon's class, Michiko delivered an oral report on "Evangeline," a lengthy, dense epic poem by American poet Henry Wadsworth Longfellow in which a character named Evangeline is expelled from her home in Acadia by the British during the French and Indian War of the mid-1700s.

Mabel Sheldon wrote in Michiko's 1944 high school yearbook:

"From the very first day when you gave that lovely 'Evangeline' report in my class, I knew you had great depths and heights in you. You have wonderful talents and the other high qualities to go with them, so I know you will go far. You will not know defeat. I'm grateful to have had you in my English class. Thank you for being what you are, Michiko. More Power to you. Lovingly, Mabel Sheldon."

Miss Sheldon encouraged Michiko to leave Gila River and go to college. Michiko's mother discouraged that ambition, questioning what good it would do her, and arguing that she should be pursuing more practical skills for a woman at that time, such as typing and shorthand.

Miss Sheldon suggested Michiko apply to Mount Holyoke College, a women's college in South Hadley, Massachusetts, established in 1837 to be the female equivalent of the then all-male Ivy League schools. Mount Holyoke's founder, schoolteacher Mary Lyon, was remembered for her inspirational words to the college's students: "Go where no one else will go, do what no one else will do."

On a pass from the Gila River camp, Michiko traveled to Phoenix to take the entrance examinations for Mount Holyoke. Before the exams, Michiko stopped at a drugstore for a soda but was refused service and asked to leave—because she looked Japanese. After two years at Gila River, where what she dreamed up she made real, Michiko again ran into the barrier of being denied due to what she looked like, because she was seen as different.

She didn't let it bother her. Seventeen-year-old Michiko was accepted to Mount Holyoke on a full scholarship: "tuition and fees

*Michi is in Phoenix for the Mount Holyoke
College entrance examination, 1944.*

plus $260 for other expenses," announced the camp newspaper. A scary thought to leave her family behind at Gila River and step into the unknown alone, but she was grateful for the Americans, like Miss Sheldon and the Relocation Council, who did make it possible for her to depart the camp and go to college.

chapter 5

From that moment on, I knew
the theatre would be my life work.
—Michi Nishiura Weglyn

MICHIKO FOUND HERSELF IN YET ANOTHER
whole new world, 2,500 miles from the Arizona desert and in New
England, among the hundreds of white, female students at Mount
Holyoke College. Some shunned her for being of Japanese descent,
the race of America's enemy; others accepted her. One had a brother
fighting the Japanese in the South Pacific, but, to Michiko, she was a
warm, close friend, a "big sister."

With the farm animals she had left behind never far from her
mind—"They were as dear to me as my sister," she would later say—
Michiko studied biology. And, as with speaking in public and writing
essays, she was good at illustrating. One of her professors admired her

drawings of animal anatomy and encouraged her to take art courses and possibly pursue a career as a medical illustrator.

As she studied art, Michiko heard about a campus-wide contest sponsored by Mount Holyoke's Dramatic Club and Dance Group to design the costumes and sets for a production of *A Midsummer Night's Dream*, William Shakespeare's play about a group of young lovers beset by bewitching fairies in a magical forest. She thought back to what seemed a lifetime ago, when she made those sweaters for the chickens, and entered the contest—and won!

Local newspaper critics lauded the production and singled out for praise Michiko's designs, which wowed the audience when the curtain went up. One reviewer wrote, "The forest set designed by Michi Nishiura stole the show. This set was stylized design and extremely effective in use of light and color."

Inspired by her success, Michiko Nishiura decided to lead a life of what she called "continued applause."

In December 1944, the U.S. government announced that all the camps holding Japanese Americans would close the following year. One reason was that Japan's military was enduring continuous defeats and was in retreat. Another was the heroic combat record of Japanese American soldiers, which had been publicized across the nation. The segregated, all-Japanese American 442nd Regimental Combat Team fought the Germans in Italy and France. It became the most

*Soldiers of the all–Japanese American 442nd Regimental
Combat Team battle the Germans in France, October 1944.*

decorated U.S. Army combat unit for its size and its length of service, with 18,143 individual medals.

The loyalty of Japanese Americans also became a case for the U.S. Supreme Court to decide. During the war years, the Court had repeatedly held that what happened to the Japanese Americans was legal and did not violate the U.S. Constitution. During late 1944, the Court heard the case of Mitsuye Endo, a young Nisei woman held at the Topaz camp in central Utah, who petitioned the Court as to why she could not return to her hometown of Sacramento, California. In this case, the U.S. Supreme Court ruled that a loyal American could no longer be detained, and the U.S. government then allowed the return of Americans of Japanese descent to the U.S. West Coast. Meanwhile, the war with Japan ended in August 1945.

Toward the end of 1945, Michiko became ill with tuberculosis, or "TB," a disease dreaded at the time, caused by infection of the lungs by mycobacterium tuberculosis bacteria traveling through the air. She suffered from a cough that wouldn't go away, blood in the mucus when she coughed, waking up in a sweat at night, fever, and weight loss. Those with TB were treated as outcasts, separated from everyone else because they had the contagious disease. In the Japanese American community, some families forbade their children from marrying into a family with a history of TB. Back then, the cure was to be confined to a tuberculosis sanatorium. By December, Michiko had been forced into receiving treatment at the Glen Gardner sanatorium in New Jersey. Because she missed too much school, she had to drop out of Mount Holyoke College.

Why this? When she was doing so well, in college on a full scholarship! What caused her to get TB? Was it the close quarters at the Gila River camp? Were her lungs weakened by the endless dust there? Or was it the pesticides she had been taught to use, without any precautions, back home on the farm?

Meanwhile, in January 1945, Michiko's parents and sister, with no California farm to return to, chose to leave Gila River by accepting work at the Seabrook Farms frozen food plant near Bridgeton, New Jersey. An industrial city, growing and processing crops since World War I, Seabrook Farms was in need of labor. The company recruited and placed ads for Japanese American workers, giving them the opportunity to leave the camps. They would have not only jobs but also a place to live, in housing on the company grounds.

After regaining her health, Michiko opted to rejoin her family. In 1946, she moved to Seabrook Farms, where she saw how her family worked and lived. Over eight hundred Japanese Americans from the camps lived in barrack-like apartments with walls without any insulation. Families like the Nishiuras from hot Gila River lived through the cold East Coast nights with ice forming inside, in the cracks in the walls. At least the latrine and bathing facilities were inside, but all those living in one building had to share the same bathroom.

Instead of barbed wire, a high, chain-link fence surrounded where

Michi and other patients recuperate from tuberculosis at the Glen Garner sanatorium in New Jersey. "The Ward D gang" Michi writes on the photo, taken about 1945.

they lived, apparently for the same purpose: to keep those living there confined. In another similarity to the camps, the children of the workers were placed in child care and attended schools inside the Seabrook grounds. Unlike with the camp mess halls, however, families cooked, and had to shop for and buy their own food at the company-run stores—at higher prices than outside.

Men were paid fifty cents an hour; women, thirty-five. Sorting beans during twelve-hour shifts, Michiko's mother's hands cracked and never healed.

Michiko knew the workers like her mother needed some relief, no matter how trivial. She approached management, asking if she could play music during the night shift, from 6 p.m. to 6 a.m., to keep the workers awake. She became the disc jockey, blaring throughout the Seabrook Farms plant the hit records of the summer of 1946, including Perry Como's "Prisoner of Love."

For Michiko, how ironic playing Perry Como's record would later seem.

chapter 6

*He turned a chronically ill tubercular
into someone productive; he nursed me
back to health again and again.*
—Michi Nishiura Weglyn,
about her husband Walter

WITH HER FASCINATION WITH THEATER,
Michiko knew she had to go to America's theater capital, New York
City. She returned to school later in 1946, this time at the city's
Barnard College, an independent women's college within Columbia
University. It was established for the same reason as Mount Holyoke
College—to provide women with college educations at schools that
would be the equivalent of those available only to men. But after
discovering the fierce competition to become a theatrical set designer,
Michiko narrowed her focus to becoming a costume designer, and
switched to the Fashion Academy of New York.

Michiko lived in Manhattan at the International House. Begun in 1924 as a place for Sunday dinners for foreign graduate students or those preparing for careers all over the world, the House provided living quarters for hundreds of students a year. The motto in stone above its entrance read, "That Brotherhood May Prevail." The House was a place for "just meeting" students from other countries.

There, in 1948, Michiko Nishiura met Walter Weglyn while he was visiting a Dutch friend who also lived there.

Walter grew up in the town of Ulm, near the city of Stuttgart in southwestern Germany. His father, Siegmund (also known as "Siego") Weglein, was a decorated soldier of the German army during World War I, who had lost a leg in combat; Walter's mother Resi served as a nurse tending to the war wounded. Approximately ninety-two thousand Jews served in the German army during World War I, with 78 percent at the front lines in combat, and twelve thousand of them killed in action. Siegmund Weglein was one of thirty-five thousand Jews decorated for heroism.

Walter was born Walter Manfred Weglein in 1926. By 1933, the Nazi Party had assumed political power and begun discriminating against, then persecuting, all the known Jews in Germany. Concentration camps for enemies of the Nazi Party had been under construction since the Nazis took power. Nazi hatred of Germany's Jewish population broke into the open in 1938 with Kristallnacht, or the "Night of Broken Glass," when Nazis and their sympathizers tore through cities and towns throughout Germany, assaulting, beating, killing Jews; vandalizing, burning, destroying Jewish businesses and synagogues.

This childhood picture of Walter is taken before World War II.

That Siegmund Weglein was a decorated World War I veteran of the German army gave him no protection from being deported to a concentration camp—he was still Jewish.

Fearing for Walter and his older brother, Heinz, Siegmund and Resi Weglein arranged to have them sent away to safety via the Kindertransport, an effort by European individuals, international religious groups, and European countries, including Britain and Holland, to transport some ten thousand Jewish children out of Germany. In 1939, twelve-year-old Walter was able to grab the last spot among a group of two thousand Jewish children escaping to Holland.

Walter rode the train from Stuttgart to Rotterdam, ending up in a camp and boardinghouse for refugee children. He then found himself fortunate to eventually be taken in by the family of a wealthy Jewish Dutch industrialist, the de Heers. But after the Nazi invasion and occupation of the Netherlands in 1940, Walter's benefactors were hauled away to a concentration camp and Walter was forced to flee. For the next three years, between 1942 and 1945, he took refuge in eleven different hiding places—including closets and ditches. Among those assisting him was a Dutch diplomat's wife, who nightly buried him under a goat stable.

Unknown to Walter was that the same year he began hiding, his parents were forced onto a train at Stuttgart and deported to the Czechoslovakian city of Terezin, into an area known as Theresienstadt. There, the Nazis packed 144,000 European Jews into a confined section of the city that served as a temporary stop on the way to the death camps, including Treblinka and Auschwitz, Poland. Starvation and disease swept through the Jewish ghetto created by the Nazis before it was liberated by the Soviet Union's Red Army in 1945.

With Allied forces driving the Nazi military out of the Netherlands in late 1944, Walter was eventually able to come out of hiding. The fate of his parents never far from his mind, he was to find out that the U.S. Army had located Siegmund and Resi Weglein at Stuttgart in June 1945. They were among the nineteen thousand who survived Theresienstadt, and the Weglein family was finally reunited. Walter also learned that he was one of only two survivors among the two thousand aboard the 1939 Kindertransport to Holland.

In 1947, Walter Weglein boarded a ship as an immigrant to America. He visited his Dutch friend—a member of a family who had taken him in when he arrived in Rotterdam via the Kindertransport. The friend introduced Walter to Michiko in the dining room of the International House. Walter, changing his name to Walter Matthys Weglyn, became a naturalized U.S. citizen in 1950. He eventually went to work as a perfume chemist for a Dutch-based company in New York, International Flavors and Fragrances.

Michi wears her engagement ring in a picture taken at the Mt. Kipp Sanatorium in 1949.

In 1949, it happened to Michiko again: another bout with tuberculosis, and this time a stay at the Mt. Kipp Sanatorium in Saranac Lake, New York. Why did this keep happening to her? She read all she could on her illness. But then something else also happened to her—Walter visited the sanatorium with a proposal of marriage.

After leaving Seabrook Farms, Michiko's parents Tomojiro and Misao and sister Tomiko had made their way back to California, settling in Los Angeles. Both the Weglein and Nishiura parents expressed skepticism about an interracial marriage, which, at that

Michi and Walter Weglyn begin their married life together, 1951.

time, was also still illegal in over half of the states in America. Michiko's mother was firmly against the marriage. However, when she met Walter, she found his manner and values—his selflessness and regard for others—to be "more Japanese than a Japanese," and she ended up loving him. On March 5, 1950, Walter Weglyn married Michiko Nishiura. The ceremony was held near Washington, DC, at the residence of Dr. A. H. Philipse, the Dutch diplomat who helped hide Walter in Holland.

Walter and Michiko decided not to have children. With the Holocaust and the incarceration of Japanese Americans still traumatic events, only a few years removed, they didn't want their children to undergo the childhoods that they had experienced.

chapter 7

Glamour is an illusion.

—Michi Nishiura Weglyn

AFTER COMPLETING HER STUDIES AT THE

Fashion Academy and marrying Walter, Michiko found that work was hard to come by for a costume designer of Japanese descent. Other Japanese Americans had the same experience: Doors closed and calls and applications went unanswered or were met with rejection. To work at some companies required labor union membership, and the unions refused to accept anyone of Japanese ancestry. Union drivers refused to drive the crops grown by Japanese-operated farms to the markets.

As with seeking employment, Japanese Americans found doors shut in their faces when inquiring about renting a home or apartment. After leaving the camps, many having lost everything they owned, they found housing wherever they could, sometimes in trailers, in boardinghouses, in the churches and the Japanese language school back in their hometowns. Those fortunate to have a home or business to return to—held in place by a trusted non-Japanese friend or neighbor who hadn't become untrustworthy and sold off all their possessions—sometimes found it vandalized, burglarized, or scrawled with graffiti about what would, or should, happen to the "Japs."

The same was true of the social clubs and service organizations outside of work. The much-decorated Japanese American U.S. Army veterans of World War II were refused membership at that time into the local posts of national veterans' organizations like the American Legion and the Veterans of Foreign Wars.

With feelings against all things Japanese still strong after the war, Americans of Japanese descent tried hard to be accepted, to blend in and not call attention to themselves, to not question what happened to them, and to put it in the past.

⁂

Michiko and Walter lived in an apartment in the Forest Hills area of the borough of Queens in New York City. Michiko left examples of her fashion illustrations with prospective employers who let her through the door. But she had little success keeping her foot in any of those doors. Was it because of what she looked like? Or was it because she had no professional experience designing costumes? And how was she to gain that experience if no one gave her a job?

One of those who let her through the door was Arthur Knorr, head producer at the Roxy Theatre. The Roxy was the legendary theater near Times Square that seated an audience of 6,214. Theater-chain operator Samuel "Roxy" Rothafel called it "the Cathedral of the Motion Picture" and had begun showing movies there in 1927. It also had a stage for live shows, and an ice rink atop the stage that was renovated in 1952 for *Ice Colorama*, an extravaganza featuring skaters in elaborate costumes. Ice-show "troupes" were known as the Choraleers, the Crystal Ballet Corps, and the Blades and Belles.

When she first approached Knorr for a job in 1950, Michiko was told, "I like your work. But, we have no job opening, now."

But on Thanksgiving Day of 1952, Michiko received a call from Arthur Knorr. He remembered her and said he needed a costumer for his upcoming show, *Crystal Circus*, to be performed over a new, neon-tube-colored ice floor. He needed sketches of her costuming ideas immediately. Instead of Thanksgiving dinner, Walter brought home a turkey drumstick for her. She ate it with one hand and sketched with the other. Knorr said in response to her sketches: "Wonderful. You're on your way to stardom."

With the show to premiere on December 22, Michiko hurriedly launched into the costuming process. She submitted her drawings and directions to the seamstress, who would assemble and sew the actual costumes. Then the wardrobe mistress made the final adjustments and readied the costumes for the performers. After the fittings on

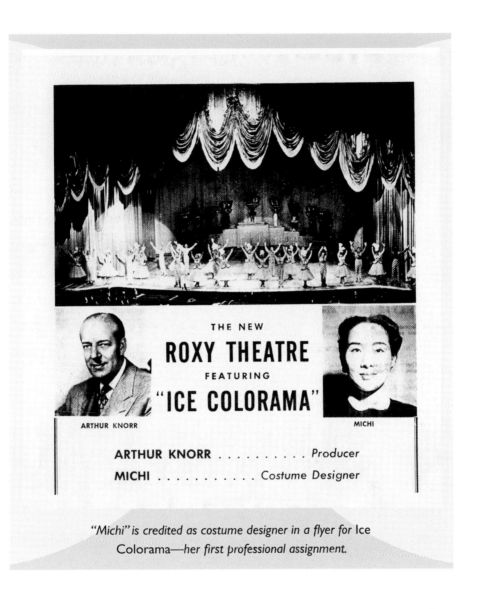

THE NEW
ROXY THEATRE
FEATURING
"ICE COLORAMA"

ARTHUR KNORR   MICHI

ARTHUR KNORR . . . . Producer

MICHI . . . . Costume Designer

"Michi" is credited as costume designer in a flyer for Ice
Colorama—*her first professional assignment.*

the performers, Michiko oversaw how her creations functioned in
action. Could the performers move and do what she or he needed
to do wearing what began as an idea?

Advertisements for "The New Roxy Theatre" featured a photograph of "Michi" as the "Costume Designer." *Crystal Circus* was a

success, and a newspaper reviewer wrote about Michi: "The girl who hadn't had a drawing lesson until she studied biology, and couldn't find a job until she found a top job, gives thanks daily now for Thanksgiving Day." Michi went on to create costumes for more *Ice Colorama* shows and characters, including "swashbuckling aerialists, daring cyclists, clowns, a wicked witch, Snow White, a Siamese golden idol and incense bearers," another newspaper reporter wrote.

Early on in her costuming career, while working for the Roxy Theatre, she had an epiphany: "I realized then that you don't have to be beautiful to get ahead in show business. The chorus girls weren't knockouts. But they did have talent, perseverance and lots of know-how on looking beautiful."

Michi's work with the Roxy Theatre led to her becoming the costume designer for other Broadway shows, including *Collector's Item*, *Hellzapoppin*, and *Hit the Trail*; and for *Skating Vanities*, a touring production featuring roller-skating-turned-ice-skating star Gloria Nord.

Michi learned how to work frantically but efficiently, scouring through New York for what she needed for her costumes—sometimes having to do so in the hour before the curtain rose! She once stood in front of a truck, refusing to let it pass unless its driver transported her and her costumes to a theater. She jumped into cabs to get to department stores like Macy's, where she dashed behind counters and started grabbing like a shoplifter, hoping to get the immediate attention of a salesperson. She attended auctions to maintain her stock of clothing and fabrics. She kept a little black book filled with the names of hundreds of New York designers, manufacturers, and suppliers, and

Always the exceptional illustrator, Michi draws her idea for a skater's costume.

details of what she could find from each. Worried she might lose the book, she wrote "Reward" on the front and back covers.

In 1954, Michi earned her first chance to work as a costume designer for a television show, *Kraft Television Theatre*. An anthology TV series with a different story and cast every week, hour-long filmed plays were shot in a New York studio at the Rockefeller Plaza. For Michi,

Michi illustrates her design for a theatrical costume.

television presented a new challenge: she had to develop her "camera eye"—to envision how those costumes would look on television, since she saw that the TV screen had a "tendency to shorten people."

That year she was also hired to design costumes for the "Copa Girls," the chorus line at New York's popular Copacabana nightclub with its Latin-themed music and decor, and at another noted New

York nightclub, La Vie en Rose, named after a popular song of the late 1940s by French singer Edith Piaf. For the costumes for both nightclubs, Michi said she used "everything from ferns to feathers."

The next year, she designed costumes for *NBC Opera: Madame Butterfly*, a TV adaptation of the Giacomo Puccini opera. Set in Japan, the story follows a Japanese woman who marries and then is forsaken by a U.S. Navy lieutenant. Michi was adamant that if the costumes were to be designed by her, they would have to be authentic. She spent hours researching, consulted with many Japanese families and a Buddhist monk, and borrowed and rented costumes from individuals in New York.

Michi learned the tricks of her trade costuming for some of the best-known names on television during the 1950s, including Eddie Fisher, Patti Page, Tony Bennett, Julius La Rosa, and Bob Crosby (brother of the famous singer and actor Bing Crosby).

The shows hosted by Page, La Rosa, and Crosby were used as summer replacements for the popular *Perry Como Show*. Como's over-fifty-year singing and hosting career started on radio in 1936 and continued on television from 1948 until 1993. In 1956, Michi began working on *The Perry Como Show* and continued during the next nine years with *Perry Como's Kraft Music Hall*, becoming the wardrobe designer for Como, all his guests, and the dancers on the weekly program.

Michi was in demand because she knew how to use clothes to make the wearer look better.

"The thing I strive for is a semblance of harmony with the anatomy," she said. "In other words, I want everything to look proportionally right. That's the first step toward glamour. If you look at the Renaissance statues, you see the proportion is beauty. And since none of us is perfect, I try to design clothes that create this harmony for the human body."

For the guests on *The Perry Como Show*, Michi designed the wardrobes for some of the biggest entertainment stars of the time, including Dinah Shore, Bob Hope, and Ginger Rogers. Every week, she performed the demanding task of dressing a new guest with what would look best. For Michi, there was always a solution.

"Take Ginger Rogers as an example," Michi said. "Ginger has a beautiful, svelte silhouette, but she has tennis arms. They photograph a little thick, and so we design special sleeves or jackets for them."

Michi knew solid colors made shorter women look taller. Beige or tan shoes made legs look longer. For shorter women, Michi said she worked for a "long-neck look" and kept bulky materials away from the neck. "No frills and fancy collars." Too short of a dress length "makes a woman look even shorter, more squat." Dark stockings on women drew attention to the legs and would "make legs conspicuous, particularly on camera. . . . Most of us average people have slightly heavy legs—and dark hose calls attention to what we shouldn't be emphasizing.

"The trick here is to achieve an uncluttered and unbroken vertical look."

Michi continued: "Light colors advance; dark colors retreat. A light-colored bathing suit hits a beach with more impact than does a red one, because it reflects the sun. This is particularly true in TV."

The men on TV also were subject to Michi's "anatomical harmony." She knew that pleats on pants made men look wider, and long suit jackets made men look "shorter and older." She had particular praise for her boss, Perry Como, who knew the tricks of Michi's trade and also had her "camera eye."

Michi said, "Don't you think that it's a testimonial to his fastidious nature that he manages to look at least 15 pounds lighter and 15 years younger on TV—and without any makeup? Who else on TV, male or female, can make that claim?"

Being a costume and wardrobe designer in the entertainment business meant a lot of fast-paced, quickly changing, hard work. However, there was a facet to it that wasn't so glamorous for an attractive woman and a woman of color. Journalists sometimes resorted to stereotypes, describing Michi as "a small, fragile beauty with fiery black eyes," or writing that "in her tight, black velvet dress, Michi looks like a doll." "Exotic is the word for Japanese-American Michi . . ."

Jack Leonard, an "insult comic" who made guest appearances on Perry Como's show from 1956 to 1964, once wagged a finger at Michi while she was on the set and said, "Ah, ya little Jap, ya started that big war." Michi's response was to try to smile, as she was uncertain how she should react.

But Como, whom Michi recalled as "so wonderful," came over to her, placed his arm around her shoulders, and responded: "Leave her alone; stop picking on her. Michi was on our side."

chapter 8

From an apolitical innocent I became
a traumatized citizen.
—Michi Nishiura Weglyn

IN 1952, THE IMMIGRANT ISSEI WERE
finally allowed to become naturalized U.S. citizens by an act of the
U.S. Congress—the McCarran-Walter Immigration and Nationality
Act. Alien Land Laws, which had previously prohibited property from
being owned by Issei "aliens ineligible to citizenship," such as Michi's
father and mother—were repealed in Oregon (1949), California
(1952), Montana (1955), and Washington (1966).

By the 1960s, Japanese Americans had for the most part recov-
ered from one of the most devastating experiences in American
history. During their time in the camps and in post–World War II
America, they had internalized slogans brought by the immigrants

from Japan: *shikata ga nai* ("it can't be helped"), *gaman* ("endure the unendurable").

With their attitude of not looking back and dealing only with the present, they worked their way into the country's lower-middle class, but still found they could go only so far. They were accepted into more occupations than before the war but, due to lingering prejudice—and barriers against people of color and women in general—reaching the top managerial and executive positions was rare.

They could live in more neighborhoods than before the war, but "redlining" continued: banks refused to issue home loans due to the race of the prospective buyer, and real estate and neighborhood rules, or "covenants," defined who—usually determined by the person's ethnicity, race, or religion—could live in a neighborhood.

However, instead of complaining and protesting, the Japanese American community made sure to protect and promote the gains it had made. It could show only its best side to the rest of America, its leaders emphasized. Loyalty, "duty to country," and becoming the best American citizens were the only acceptable means of conduct. The Japanese American Citizens League (JACL), a national organization founded in 1930 to advocate for the civil rights of Japanese Americans, worked on changing or eliminating discriminatory laws, including the Alien Land Laws, and obtaining the right for the Issei to become American citizens. It adopted as its motto "Better Americans in a Greater America."

To keep its members in line, a sort of self-policing evolved within

Japanese American communities to ensure that one member did not tarnish the reputation of the entire group. To be an excellent student in school was expected, and crime and juvenile delinquency in the Japanese American community were not tolerated. As Michi would later write, "respect for authority was strongly reinforced." Americans of Japanese descent had learned the hard lesson, they thought, of what happened when they called attention to themselves. Only "good things" that Japanese Americans had achieved since the war would be highlighted. No one had better dare to "rock the boat." "Don't make waves!"

As Michi continued to work as the wardrobe designer for *The Perry Como Show*, she formed her own company, Michi Associates, Ltd., to manufacture and rent out costumes to satisfy individual requests for her clothing designs. She also designed for *The Jimmy Dean Show*, featuring the country recording artist who had his first hit record in 1953, and in 1965 Michi worked on the costumes for the RCA—Radio Corporation of America—exhibit at the New York World's Fair. The RCA showcase featured a recent invention—color TV. When Perry Como's show moved to Los Angeles in 1966, Michi chose to stay in New York. She continued with TV wardrobe work, including a special with the legendary dancer and actor Gene Kelly, and a series with actor Robert Morse.

At home, Michi and Walter watched the events of the decade unfold on the nightly news and in newspapers, *Life* magazine, and other news periodicals of the time.

Century-old segregation laws mandating "whites only" and "colored only" separation in places for public use, such as restrooms, restaurants, theaters, parks, swimming pools, and public transportation, had begun to be challenged by the African American civil rights movement. Protesters marched and sat in seats supposedly reserved for "whites only." During nonviolent strikes, pickets, and marches, African American protesters were screamed at and beaten by white counterprotesters and law enforcement.

On the other side of the world, the U.S. military was engaged in combat with the North Vietnamese army and its guerrilla supporters, culminating in about half a million U.S. military personnel serving in South Vietnam by the end of the decade. To meet its manpower needs, the military draft was reinstituted in the United States: all males reaching age eighteen were required to register with the Selective Service, the federal agency handling the draft. Demonstrations and protests against the war and the draft erupted across the country in the late 1960s, sometimes resulting in deadly clashes between the protesters and both law enforcement and supporters of the war.

Coverage of the war was constant on TV sets in living rooms throughout America, showing Vietnamese civilians caught in the middle and suffering the most. Michi would later describe what she watched then as "when the use of technological savagery on the lives, habitats, and ecosystem of a small Asian nation was shocking the entire civilized world."

In April 1968, civil rights leader Rev. Dr. Martin Luther King Jr.

was assassinated, shot and killed while speaking from a motel balcony in Memphis. In June, an assassin gunned down Robert Kennedy, the former U.S. attorney general and then U.S. senator, in a Los Angeles hotel kitchen as he campaigned to become the U.S. president. During that summer's Democratic National Convention, unrestrained Chicago police, with tape over their badges to obscure identification, assaulted and beat protesters outside the convention hall.

America was embroiled in chaos and violence at home and abroad, and skepticism began to rise about its government and its leaders. That was when Michi experienced what she described as "the transition that took place within me." She said, "I was enraged by a democracy's flagrant disregard for elemental human rights, especially as they related to ethnicity and skin color, and by America's shocking disregard for a reverence for life which we had long been taught to hold sacred."

During that pivotal 1968 for Michi and the country, she had read the book *While Six Million Died: A Chronicle of American Apathy.* First published in 1967, it was written by Arthur D. Morse, a television news reporter and producer who had resigned from his job at CBS to research and write his account of why the U.S. government had been reluctant to rescue and let into the country Jewish refugees fleeing the Holocaust during World War II.

Racism and anti-Semitism had woven their way through America long before the war. A million immigrants from eastern and southern Europe, which included Italy, poured into America during the early 1900s. Like immigrants from Asia, they were viewed as the "other," with languages and cultures regarded as so different that they couldn't be assimilated into American society. An immigration commission appointed by the U.S. government in 1907 supported the notion that "southern and eastern Europeans were racially inferior to northern and western Europeans."

After World War I, the U.S. government favored policies of isolationism—to stay out of the affairs and conflicts of other countries in the world—and sought to limit immigrants coming to America. The Immigration Act of 1924 effectively halted any further immigration from Japan. With a 1929 quota on immigrants established, the U.S. government limited all immigration to 153,774 "aliens" a year, with more than half of that quota reserved for applications for immigration from England and Ireland.

Those immigration laws, Morse wrote, "had been directed at nineteenth-century abuses but now kept out twentieth-century Jews."

During the 1930s, the United States and the rest of the world began to hear news of Nazi persecution of the Jewish population in Germany. President Roosevelt, his secretary of state Cordell Hull, and his State Department remained indifferent, refusing to become involved in the internal affairs of Germany. That same indifference extended to other sectors in America, such as sports, with the American Olympic Committee deciding to attend the 1936 Olympic Games in Berlin despite knowledge of what was going on under Hitler's rule.

Morse wrote, "Failure to protest was the first in a long series of refusals to respond *in any manner*. One might describe the American response to Nazi racism as an almost co-ordinated series of inactions" (Morse's italics).

By the time of America's entry into World War II, persecution of the Jewish population in Germany and conquered European countries had turned into extermination. The Roosevelt administration, even after consulting with other nations of the world, especially Britain, still held back from a policy of rescuing European Jews from the Holocaust. The administration's rationale was that allowing a large number of them into the United States would be a "nullification or evasion" of U.S. immigration quota laws; would run counter to "protecting the nation against an invasion by radicals and foreign agents"; and, as Assistant Secretary of State Breckinridge Long wrote, would "lend color to the charges of Hitler that we are fighting this war on account of and instigation of our Jewish citizens."

President Roosevelt also had his own political future to consider—being reelected as president of the United States.

Morse wrote of the president: "Since he was afraid that the Jewish issue was a political liability, he helped to doom European Jewry by inaction even as he proclaimed America as the asylum for the oppressed."

Michi said that when she finished reading *While Six Million Died*, she was stunned by the "appalling apathy and callousness of our government." Then comparisons began forming in her mind. What Arthur D. Morse had discovered and uncovered—was this somehow connected to what she and 110,000 other Japanese Americans went through during that same war?

Did the American government, including President Roosevelt, hide the real reason her parents had lost their jobs and everything they had toiled decades for, why she had to leave behind her beloved animal friends? What was the real reason she had been forced into the overcrowded Gila River camp, leading to tuberculosis and never graduating from college? Had it been not for the safety and security of her country but only because of her race—and for politicians to get elected or reelected by doing what was most popular at the time?

One day in April 1968, as she watched the news on television soon after the assassination of Martin Luther King Jr., came the moment that would change the direction of Michi's life. Asked about rumors that African Americans would be put in concentration camps, Attorney General Ramsey Clark answered, as Michi recalled: "We never have had, do not now have and will not ever have concentration camps here."

Clark's words "startled me into disbelief," Michi said. "His blatant untruth convinced me that uncovering the probable lies of our long revered wartime President Franklin Roosevelt would surely lead me to the truth as to why we innocents had been consigned to prison camps."

But what could she do about it? She was a costume and wardrobe designer, not a researcher and writer. She didn't even have a college degree.

For her husband, Walter, what was in *While Six Million Died* was, of course, also personal. He talked with Michi about her outrage and encouraged her. If she wanted to uncover the facts, then she should commit herself to doing so. If she didn't do it, who would?

Michi recalled her parents never saying anything negative about President Roosevelt, despite all they had endured. But she felt it had to be done. There was something out there, buried somewhere! She would do her detective work and not be swayed by what others—including her fellow Japanese Americans—thought. Even if it meant rocking the boat.

And, as Michi said later, she had another reason: "I knew I was more than an exotic, Oriental doll."

chapter 9

*For an untrained researcher it was
agonizing to decide how to proceed.*

—Michi Nishiura Weglyn

THE ENORMITY OF WHAT SHE WAS ABOUT
to confront began with: Where to start?

Of course, where anyone would start: the library . . .

Michi left crowded Fifth Avenue in Manhattan and ascended the
steps, entered through the marble arches, and walked down the
echoing halls of the New York Public Library. She found the few
books on the World War II Japanese American—and her own—
experience. But Michi felt strongly that more had to exist about the
Roosevelt administration's actions during the war—especially after
having read *While Six Million Died.* Those few books that she found
cited a common source: the Franklin D. Roosevelt Library in Hyde
Park, New York.

Michi took the two-hour ride from New York City north along the Hudson River to Hyde Park. She walked through the well-manicured grounds, past the bust of the president, and into the library's archives—shelves of black boxes containing some seventeen million pages of documents. Narrowing her search with questions to the library staff, Michi sifted through memorandums, letters back and forth between the president, his cabinet members, and other govern-ment officials, until she found what she had been looking for, and what she had suspected had to be there: a report buried by the Roosevelt administration and not made public until after the war, when it was made known at an obscure government hearing and never hit the newspapers.

In the fall of 1941, fearing an attack by the Japanese military on U.S. armed forces, President Roosevelt ordered Curtis B. Munson, special representative of the State Department, to conduct an inves-tigation into the loyalty of those of Japanese descent living in the United States. During October and November of that year, Munson performed four weeks of interviews and fact-finding up and down the West Coast and Hawaii, then issued his twenty-five-page report.

Examining the Japanese by their generations, he concluded:

The Issei, immigrants from Japan, on average fifty-five to sixty-five years old in 1941, were "considerably weakened in their loyalty to Japan by the fact they have chosen to make this their home and brought up their children here. They expect to die here." He added that "their wealth accumulated by hard labor is here, and many would have become American citizens had they been allowed to do so." He also noted that the Issei were "almost exclusively a farmer, a fisherman or a small businessman."

The Nisei, children of the Issei, on average eighteen years old at the time, "have received their whole education in the United States and usually, in spite of discrimination against them and a certain amount of insults accumulated through the years from irresponsible elements, show a pathetic eagerness to be Americans."

For the Kibei, the Nisei born in America but educated in Japan, Munson wrote, "The Kibei are considered the most dangerous element." He noted, however, that many of those who visited Japan after their early American education "come back with added loyalty to the United States. In fact it is a saying that all a Nisei needs is a trip to Japan to make a loyal American out of him. The American educated Japanese is a boor in Japan and treated as a foreigner."

Munson did go on to write: "There are still Japanese in the United States who will tie dynamite around their waist and make a human bomb out of themselves. We grant this, but today they are few." He summarized the Nisei as "universally estimated from 90 to 98 percent loyal to the United States," "not Japanese in culture," and "foreigners to Japan."

Munson concluded, "After interview after interview piled up, those bringing in results began to call it the same old tune. The story was all the same. There is no Japanese 'problem' on the Coast. There will be no armed uprising of Japanese. There will undoubtedly be some sabotage financed by Japan and executed largely by imported agents . . .

"For the most part the local Japanese are loyal to the United States or, at worst, hope by remaining quiet they can avoid concentration camps or irresponsible mobs. We do not believe that they would be at the least any more disloyal than any other racial group in the United States with whom we went to war. Those being here are on the spot and they *know it*" (Munson's italics).

For the Japanese on Hawaii, Munson found the same:

"The consensus of opinion is that there will be no racial uprising of the Japanese in Honolulu. The first generation, as on the Coast, are ideologically and culturally closest to Japan. Though many of them speak no English, or at best only pidgin English, it is considered that the big bulk of them will be loyal. . . . The second generation is estimated as approximately ninety-eight percent loyal."

Munson issued his findings "with the full cooperation of Naval and Army Intelligence and the FBI," which he revealed had had people of Japanese descent under surveillance for ten to fifteen years prior to 1941. Michi also found documents that showed that the FBI and U.S. Naval Intelligence did not agree with the planned forced removal and imprisonment of all Japanese Americans. FBI director J. Edgar Hoover wrote to the president that such an action would be "based primarily upon public political pressure rather than upon factual data," since his agency had detained or had under surveillance those suspected of any type of threat to the United States. Naval authorities preferred that the determination of loyalty and detainment be conducted on an individual basis, and judgment not passed on the entire group.

After the attack on Pearl Harbor in December, Munson followed up his report with a letter to the president: "Your reporter, fully believing that his reports are still good after the attack, makes the following observations about handling the Japanese 'problem' on the West Coast."

Munson began: "The loyal Japanese citizens should be encouraged by a statement from high government authority and public attitude toward them outlined." He continued that Japanese Americans, particularly the Nisei, should be allowed to assist the wartime civilian agencies such as the Red Cross, the United Service Organizations (USO), and Civilian Defense, and that "investigated Nisei" be allowed to work in the defense industries such as shipbuilding and aircraft plants. "The Nisei should work with and among white persons, and be made to feel he is welcome on a basis of equality," Munson wrote.

Upon reading Munson's words, Michi must have thought how different her life, and the lives of 110,000 others of Japanese descent, would have been, had the president followed his recommendations.

From Hyde Park, Michi's detective work led to the next obvious place where evidence was stored: the National Archives in Washington, DC. She made regular train trips there from New York City, arriving at 9 a.m., when the doors opened at the research entrance on Pennsylvania Avenue. Searching through volumes of catalogs and questioning librarians, she requested boxes of files, then sifted through endless folders and papers. She took a break only at midday to eat the carefully wrapped sandwich that Walter—always concerned about Michi's health—had reminded her to bring. She spent all the time she could in the research room, waiting in line to use the copying machine and staying until the archives closed.

On the over three-hour ride back to New York from Washington, DC, Michi might have wondered, with her tired eyes, what she had gotten herself into. Was it all worth it? What would she do with the growing stacks of copied documents? But after what she had discovered so far, and recalling what she had gone through during her lifetime, there was no quitting.

And Walter encouraged her to keep going.

As Michi huddled with her research, American history was being made right there in Washington, DC. In 1972, burglars were caught rifling through the Democratic National Committee headquarters in the city's Watergate building. That incident led to congressional investigations and hearings, connecting the burglars to close associates and staff members of President Richard M. Nixon who were seeking information on the president's political opponents and enemies. In 1974, with his contribution to the cover-up of the conspiracy confirmed, Nixon became the first president in American history to resign from his office.

To Michi, did what she was looking into—what top leaders of the U.S. government were capable of—then seem even more possible?

As she would say later, when war hysteria on the U.S. West Coast was cited as one of the causes of her and other Japanese Americans being forced into the World War II camps, "the hysteria was actually in the White House!"

She also made trips out west to libraries at the University of California at Los Angeles, and the University of California–Berkeley. Around that same time, American college-age students largely of Chinese, Japanese, and Filipino descent began to pattern themselves after those who would no longer be called "Negro" but instead "Black" and then "African American." The young activists denounced "Oriental" as an outdated European label and adopted "Asian" instead. They advocated self-pride and encouraged a search for their own histories not influenced or omitted by a lifetime of Eurocentric versions. The Sansei, the third generation of Japanese Americans, the children of Michi's Nisei generation, began asking their parents about the missing pieces in their family histories, especially about those erased years their parents would refer to only as "camp."

"Many Japanese Americans have been quiet about the internment for all these years because it's still painful to talk about what happened to us," Michi said.

In 1970, Edison Uno, a San Francisco Bay Area college educator specializing in the history of the wartime camps, began advocating the then-audacious idea of "redress": that the U.S. government should monetarily compensate the victims of incarceration during World War II.

Uno, also a busy civil rights activist, helped lead the successful

Edison Uno, who first proposes "redress" for Japanese Americans affected by U.S. government actions during World War II. Photo taken in January 1974.

movement in 1971 to repeal the Emergency Detention Act. This 1950 federal law authorized the detention of those who, based on "reasonable ground," would "probably engage in" acts of espionage or sabotage when the president had declared an "internal security emergency." The law also authorized the Justice Department to construct facilities (concentration camps) to detain suspected individuals. Rumors and suspicion circulated in the late 1960s that the act would be used to target civil rights activists, leaders of the African American "Black Pride" movement, or antiwar protesters—leading to the reporter's question to U.S. Attorney General Ramsey Clark and his reply that sparked Michi on her mission.

Edison Uno's "redress" concept was at first rebuffed as too "radical," including by the Japanese American Citizens League with its emphasis on steadfast American citizenship and cooperation. To challenge the U.S. government to admit it had committed a wrong in the past, and to compensate those wronged with cash payments, would "rock the boat." Uno labeled himself a "non-conforming progressive Nisei."

But during the 1970s the concept began to catch on in the national Japanese American community. First formally introduced by a Seattle chapter, the once-reluctant JACL eventually adopted a national campaign to seek redress. Under its proposal, compensation for each Japanese American confined to the camps during World War II was set at $25,000—still only a tiny fraction of what they had actually lost from 1942 through 1945. The money amount was more of a token payment, a way for the U.S. government to reinforce its recognition that it had committed a wrong with something more than just the words of an apology.

While Edison Uno rocked the boat in public, his kindred spirit, Michi Nishiura Weglyn, labored on in private. She began to convert all the research she had conducted into a coherent book. When she began writing—typing on a portable Royal Companion typewriter—she didn't just repeat the facts she had discovered. Michi threw herself into it as a Japanese American writing a nonfiction history about the World War II camps—from one who had actually lived through that experience.

She didn't hold back.

chapter 10

My God, they were lying to us!

—Michi Nishiura Weglyn

MICHI BEGAN WITH HER KEY PIECE OF

evidence: the Munson Report.

"Evidence would indicate that the Munson Report was shared only by the State, War, and Navy departments," she wrote. Yet despite the report's conclusions, she continued, Secretary of State Cordell Hull, Secretary of War Henry L. Stimson, and Secretary of the Navy Frank Knox "were to end up being the most determined proponents of evacuation" of Japanese Americans from the West Coast.

Michi found a February 5, 1942, memorandum from Stimson to the president, in which Stimson conveyed that his War Department had given the Munson Report "careful study and consideration" since being sent the report on November 8, 1941.

Michi concluded: "This meant that the General Staff had fully

three months to study, circulate, review, and analyze the conten[...]
the report." But because the Munson Report had been conc[...]
"few, if any, realized how totally distorted was the known truth i[...]
internment hysterics emanating from the military." The exce[...]
were the naval intelligence service and the FBI. "Both serv[...]
their credit, are on record as having opposed the President's
for evacuation."

Michi went on to write about why the forced removal and the
camps still occurred:

"Since much of Munson's documentation for the President read
more like a tribute to those of Japanese ancestry than a need for
locking them up, the question remains: Had the President, having
perceived the racist character of the American public, deliberately
acquiesced to the clearly punitive actions knowing it would be rous-
ingly effective for the flagging home-front morale?"

Michi had discovered that before the United States removed and
incarcerated its own Japanese Americans from the West Coast, it had
pressured fourteen Latin American countries to round up and deport
those within their borders who were considered "potentially dangerous
to hemispheric security." A memo from Secretary of State Cordell Hull
to the president urging the continued deportation of "all the Japanese"
for internment in the United States concluded: "Continue our efforts
to remove from South and Central America all the dangerous Germans
and Italians still there, together with their families."

"The precise wording of the directive is significant," Michi
wrote. "Note the qualifying prerequisite, *dangerous*, in references to

In a meeting of the Roosevelt administration cabinet, December 1941,
the president is seated at the center of the table. Next to him to the right
are Secretary of State Cordell Hull and Attorney General Francis Biddle.
Across the table are Secretary of War Henry Stimson (in uniform) and
behind him (farthest left) Secretary of the Interior Harold Ickes.

hostages-to-be of German and Italian nationalities. In Hull's implied suggestion of more discriminating treatment of non-Oriental Axis nationals, while calling for wholesale removal—dangerous or harmless—of 'all the Japanese,' evidence again lies tellingly exposed of racial bias then lurking in high and rarefied places in the nation's capital."

The Japanese Latin Americans were to be used as what Michi described as "barter reserve": hostages who could be traded as part of prisoner exchanges for Americans being held by the Japanese military.

Not all of President Roosevelt's cabinet members agreed with the detention of Japanese from other countries, or the impending strategy to remove and detain those of Japanese descent in America—73 percent of them born in America, and therefore American citizens.

Michi found evidence in the Franklin D. Roosevelt Library that U.S. Attorney General Francis Biddle and Secretary of the Interior Harold Ickes were disturbed by what was happening and what was to come. Attorney General Biddle, in a letter to the president, argued that the impending forced removal could be a violation of civil rights guaranteed in the U.S. Constitution. He also protested the exclusion and removal as motivated by economic gain and greed by special interests and those who "would welcome their removal from good farm land and the elimination of their competition."

However, advocates for the forced removal and incarceration of those of Japanese descent included the president; Secretary of War Stimson; Assistant Secretary of War John J. McCloy; Lt. Gen. John L. DeWitt, U.S. Army commander of the Pacific Coast area; and Col. Karl R. Bendetsen of the general staff.

The advocates brought in Bendetsen, a lawyer from the West Coast, to engineer the mass removal without being in conflict with the U.S. Constitution. Bendetsen devised the means: to circumvent, or go around, the Constitution by taking the expulsion out of the hands of the Justice Department and placing the responsibility into those of the U.S. Army—to make it a military matter instead of a legal one. The president would issue an executive order, authorizing the secretary of war to designate "military areas" from which all persons without government permission to remain would be excluded as a matter of "military necessity." The order would require the immediate removal of and deny reentry to those without that permission.

When President Roosevelt issued his Executive Order 9066, there was no mention of persons of Japanese descent. But in what was to become over forty pages of endnotes, Michi cited a letter in which Attorney General Biddle pointed out to the president that, as evident in communications between General DeWitt, Assistant Secretary of War McCloy, and Colonel Bendetsen, the order was "never intended to apply to Italians and Germans."

The U.S. Congress then passed Public Law No. 503, which made the violation of any restrictions in a "military area" punishable as a federal offense. In 1944, the U.S. Supreme Court heard the case of Fred Korematsu, a Nisei who refused to be removed from his hometown of Oakland, California. The Court upheld the legality of the Japanese American exclusion, removal, and incarceration due to "the real military dangers which were present."

Michi concluded: "Clearly, the lofty judiciary, like Congress, was

EXECUTIVE ORDER

- - - - - - -

AUTHORIZING THE SECRETARY OF WAR TO PRESCRIBE MILITARY AREAS

WHEREAS the successful prosecution of the war requires every possible protection against espionage and against sabotage to national-defense material, national-defense premises, and national-defense utilities as defined in Section 4, Act of April 20, 1918, 40 Stat. 533, as amended by the Act of November 30, 1940, 54 Stat. 1220, and the Act of August 21, 1941, 55 Stat. 655 (U. S. C., Title 50, Sec. 104):

NOW, THEREFORE, by virtue of the authority vested in me as President of the United States, and Commander in Chief of the Army and Navy, I hereby authorize and direct the Secretary of War, and the Military Commanders whom he may from time to time designate, whenever he or any designated Commander deems such action necessary or desirable, to prescribe military areas in such places and of such extent as he or the appropriate Military Commander may determine, from which any or all persons may be excluded, and with respect to which, the right of any person to enter, remain in, or leave shall be subject to whatever restrictions the Secretary of War or the appropriate Military

President Roosevelt issues Executive Order 9066 (first page shown) to exclude persons from "military areas."

totally unaware of the Munson certification of loyalty. . . . By the High Court's majority decision (6–3) vindicating the mass forcible removals on the basis of a fictitious military necessity, the Supreme Court, the Congress, and the President had coalesced as 'accomplices' in one of history's most remarkable legalizations of official illegality."

Michi continued, disclosing then-little-known facts she uncovered during her research. "Repression was applied, one small step at a time," she began a chapter describing what occurred leading up to the removal of "any or all persons" of Japanese ancestry, including the American-born, mandated by the executive order. "First came the roundup of suspect aliens; the freezing of bank accounts, the seizure of contraband, the drastic limitation on travel, curfew, and other restrictive measures of increasing severity."

Michi described the "Third Reich harshness" of the orders of Col. Bendetsen, who determined and enforced the rules of the executive order. Even for multiracial "infants abandoned in orphanages," she noted, the colonel ruled that "if they have one drop of Japanese blood in them, they must go to camp."

And then there was the question of why there was no mass expulsion of those of Japanese ancestry from Hawaii, where the attack on Pearl Harbor took place. Michi located documents showing that, although the president and Navy Secretary Knox applied pressure for this to occur, the U.S. military and civilian leaders in Hawaii were reluctant to carry it out, particularly given the proven loyalty of the 10,000 Japanese Hawaiians who volunteered for the U.S. Army. Roosevelt and Knox then called for expulsion of up to 20,000 of the "most dangerous," which eventually dwindled to 1,037 "potentially dangerous" being removed to the mainland.

Another key factor was that Japanese Hawaiians constituted more than a third of the Hawaiian labor force. Even Assistant War Secretary McCloy, who was in charge of the entire "evacuation," joined Hawaiian authorities in "discouraging the called-for transplantation which could topple the island economy if undertaken without sending in an equivalent labor force of comparable skill and experience," Michi wrote.

In mainland America, labor also proved critical, as those who worked on farms left for higher-paying defense-industry jobs such as at shipbuilding yards and airplane factories in the cities. To save the farm crops, the War Relocation Authority let Japanese Americans out of the camps, with ten thousand volunteering to harvest—and credited with saving—the sugar beet crops in Idaho, Montana, Utah, and Wyoming during fall 1942.

Michi learned that there were non-Japanese individuals and organizations that opposed the forced removal and incarceration and helped Japanese Americans, including the Quakers, whom she described as "sterling Americans." However, there were also groups that might have been expected to but didn't, such as the American Civil Liberties Union (ACLU). The national organization founded to advocate for the civil rights of Americans, Michi wrote, "timidly" took the position that President Roosevelt's Executive Order 9066 "fell quite within the proper limits of the President's war powers."

Individual ACLU attorneys disagreed with their organization's stance and aided Japanese Americans in legal cases. Michi typed: "But had it not been for the stunning indifference of the citizenry everywhere—the racist nature of society in general—the mass subjugation of a minority could not have been made possible.

"The near absence of protest had enabled the Army to proceed swiftly, smoothly, and without a hitch."

In the Franklin D. Roosevelt Library, Michi found more correspondence between the president and Interior Secretary Harold Ickes. With the camps being built on federally owned land, the camps and the War Relocation Authority were placed in the control of Ickes's Department of the Interior. He spotted trouble ahead and wrote to the president:

"Native-born Japanese who first accepted with philosophical understanding the decision of the Government to round up and take far inland all of the Japanese along the Pacific Coast, regardless of their degree of loyalty, have pretty generally been disappointed with the treatment that they have been accorded." He continued, "The result has been the gradual turning of thousands of well-meaning and loyal Japanese into angry prisoners."

By December 1942, the anger of some could no longer be contained. At Manzanar, in east-central California, approximately ten thousand Japanese Americans, largely from the Los Angeles area, were crammed into a camp one square mile in size. Laborers at the camp began organizing for better working conditions.

Harry Ueno, the Kibei leader of the Kitchen Workers Union, publicly accused the non-Japanese camp staff of pilfering precious eggs, meat, and sugar. A JACL leader accused of being an informant, supplying the names of alleged "troublemakers" to the camp administration, was found severely beaten around the same time. The administration held Ueno responsible, apprehending him and holding him in a jail outside Manzanar, with other union leaders held in the camp jail.

During the night of December 6, a seething crowd of Manzanar residents formed outside of the camp jail, demanding the release of those being held there, and of Harry Ueno. During the ensuing chaos, the camp's military police fired into the crowd, killing one and injuring nine, with one of those later dying from his wounds. The camp administration responded by removing sixteen of the labor advocates from Manzanar, placing them with "troublemakers" from other camps at separate prisons located near Moab, Utah, and Leupp, Arizona.

The reasons given for holding people at separate, more heavily guarded prisons, away from their families in the main WRA camps, included making public statements of disloyalty to the United States, influencing and instigating fellow laborers to cease work and protest, intimidating or threatening those considered informers for the camp administration, or appearing in any way to favor the enemy from Japan.

But Michi found that those confined to these prisons included a father of fifteen children "suffering from a chronic illness and mental condition." Another was a boy who, after his father had committed suicide in one of the camps, "had written a bitter essay which had fallen into the hands of authorities."

"Repression, hastily applied," Michi wrote, for "the slightest political misfeasance. . . .

"By a peculiar morality of the time in regard to the 'Japanese,' the traditional presumption of innocence was conveniently transformed into a presumption of guilt. . . . Even when the innocence of the victims became apparent, it was cynically determined by Washington that the men should remain 'separated'—the cruelest of punishment for a people bereft of everything, for whom family relationships were the only consolation left."

Michi's husband, Walter, constantly read all that she wrote. He encouraged her to stick to the truth—what was actually revealed by what she had uncovered—even though it flew in the face of what was popularly known and accepted.

"Walter is my most exacting critic and mentor," Michi said, and she was propelled "because of the critical feedback he gave me and his determination that I must expose the lies used to justify that atrocity."

chapter 11

What I wanted to do was
to break new ground.
—Michi Nishiura Weglyn

IN ADDITION TO MASS EXPULSION FROM

their homes and businesses, a second devastating event for Japanese Americans during World War II was what became known as the U.S. government's "loyalty questionnaire" and "registration."

"Ignoring the hurts, the wounds, the injuries inflicted in pitiless succession," Michi wrote, "Washington had suddenly decided that now was the time to give all detainees in the camps (excluding children under seventeen) an opportunity to concretely register their fundamental loyalty as a group by having each swear his or her unqualified allegiance to the United States."

In February 1943, the WRA presented Japanese Americans in the camps with a list of twenty-eight questions, beginning with requests

FORM APPROVED
BUDGET BUREAU No. 33-R045-43

(LOCAL BOARD DATE STAMP WITH CODE)

STATEMENT OF UNITED STATES CITIZEN OF JAPANESE ANCESTRY

1. ....
(Surname)   (English given name)   (Japanese given name)

    (a) Alias ....

2. Local selective service board ....
(Number)

    ....
(City)   (County)   (State)

3. Date of birth .... Place of birth ....

4. Present address ....
(Street)   (City)   (State)

5. Last two addresses at which you lived 3 months or more (exclude residence at relocation center and at assembly center):

    .... From .... To ....

    .... From .... To ....

6. Sex .... Height .... Weight ....

7. Are you a registered voter? .... Year first registered ....

    Where? .... Party ....

8. Marital status .... Citizenship of wife .... Race of wife ....

9. ....
(Father's Name)   (Town or Ken)   (State or Country)   (Occupation)
(Birthplace)

10. ....
(Mother's Name)   (Town or Ken)   (State or Country)   (Occupation)
(Birthplace)

In items 11 and 12, you need not list relatives other than your parents, your children, your brothers and sisters. For each person give name; relationship to you (such as father); citizenship; complete address; occupation.

11. Relatives in the United States (if in military service, indicate whether a selectee or volunteer):

    (a) ....
(Name)   (Relationship to you)   (Citizenship)

    ....
(Complete address)   (Occupation)   (Volunteer or selectee)

    (b) ....
(Name)   (Relationship to you)   (Citizenship)

    ....
(Complete address)   (Occupation)   (Volunteer or selectee)

    (c) ....
(Name)   (Relationship to you)   (Citizenship)

    ....
(Complete address)   (Occupation)   (Volunteer or selectee)

DSS Form 304A
(1-23-43)
(If additional space is necessary, attach sheets)
16—32565-1

Pictured are the first and last pages of the "loyalty questionnaire," which would create turmoil in the camps.

23. List contributions you have made to any society, organization, or club:

Organization	Place	Amount	Date

24. List magazines and newspapers to which you have subscribed or have customarily read:

....

....

....

....

....

....

25. To the best of your knowledge, was your birth ever registered with any Japanese governmental agency for the purpose of

establishing a claim to Japanese citizenship? ....

    (a) If so registered, have you applied for cancelation of such registration? ....
                                                         (Yes or no)

    When? .... Where? ....

26. Have you ever applied for repatriation to Japan? ....

27. Are you willing to serve in the armed forces of the United States on combat duty, wherever ordered? ....

28. Will you swear unqualified allegiance to the United States of America and faithfully defend the United States from any or all attack by foreign or domestic forces, and forswear any form of allegiance or obedience to the Japanese emperor, or any

other foreign government, power, or organization? ....

....	....
(Date)	(Signature)

NOTE.—Any person who knowingly and wilfully falsifies or conceals a material fact or makes a false or fraudulent statement or representation in any matter within the jurisdiction of any department or agency of the United States is liable to a fine of not more than $10,000 or 10 years' imprisonment, or both.

U. S. GOVERNMENT PRINTING OFFICE   16—32565-1

for information about activities before ending up in the camp: past addresses, employment history, involvement with and contributions to clubs and organizations, relatives in the United States and Japan, knowledge of the Japanese language. Question 27 read:

"Are you willing to serve in the armed forces of the United States on combat duty wherever ordered?"

Question 28 asked: "Will you swear unqualified allegiance to the United States of America and faithfully defend the United States from any or all attack by foreign or domestic forces, and forswear any form of allegiance or obedience to the Japanese emperor, to any other foreign government, power or organization?"

Answering yes to both cleared the Japanese American respondent to be issued a "Citizen's Indefinite Leave" card and permanently depart the camp for any location in the United States—except for the West Coast, still the restricted "military area" within what was designated as the Western Defense Command.

Question 27 was straightforward enough, but question 28 confused those required to answer. Many saw it as two questions in one, with the first half again being straightforward but the second half confounding. The young, often teenage, Nisei asked how they could "forswear any form of allegiance or obedience to the Japanese emperor" when, living in America and raised as Americans all their lives, they never had any "allegiance or obedience" to begin with. To them, answering yes would also be an admission that they previously had an allegiance to the emperor of Japan. For their parents, the immigrant Issei who were prohibited from becoming American citizens, answering yes to question 28 would leave them without citizenship in either Japan or America. How the two questions were answered starkly divided those in the camps—divisions that, in some cases, lasted for the rest of their lives.

For the Nisei, answering yes to both questions also meant being able to volunteer for the U.S. Army. At the time of the attack on Pearl Harbor, about five thousand Nisei and Kibei were serving in the U.S. armed forces. After the attack, they were turned down when volunteering to serve (except in Hawaii), and by early 1942 they were classified by the Selective Service as "IV-C," or "enemy alien." They could not volunteer for or be drafted by the U.S. military. Those already in the military—mostly in the army—in some cases were separated from the other soldiers and had their weapons taken away. But by February 1943, President Roosevelt announced that a separate and segregated "Japanese Combat Team" would be formed, and called for Nisei volunteers from the ten WRA camps. Army recruiters appeared in the camps that month—the same month that Japanese Americans were presented with the loyalty questionnaire.

After all that had happened to the Japanese Americans held in the camps, the recruiters were met with suspicion and distrust. Sometimes hostile arguments broke out among those in the camps about whether to volunteer or not. "The colossal folly of recording each inmate's attitudes toward America in a concentration camp, *after all the damage had been done*, was to be compounded by the WRA's decision to conduct the mass registration in conjunction with an Army recruitment drive in the centers" (Michi's italics).

Michi was not yet seventeen years old at that time at the Gila River camp, but her parents must have answered yes to both questions in order to be able to depart to Seabrook Farms. In retrospect, Michi wrote about the confusion and turmoil that swirled around her then:

"Why the oath-taking now when it could have been done before the evacuation? Why this need for proof, proof, and more proof? Couldn't the incessant 'Jap's a Jap' propaganda, depicting them as nothing more than vile, debased descendants of monkey men, be ground to a halt? Couldn't the President simply reinstate them in the eyes of the American public by telling the nation that the Nisei and their parents have committed no wrong, that they should be treated fairly and squarely, like those of German and Italian ancestry?"

What followed the "loyalty questionnaire" was the "weeding out" of people whom War Secretary Stimson labeled as "traitors" and "rotten apples." Some of those who replied no to both questions (known as the "No-No Boys") became outspoken on the registration issue and were "proving irksome by their brazen exercise of the freedom of speech," Michi wrote. Senate Resolution 166, passed in July 1943, ordered that these "disloyals" be removed from their current camps and sent to the Tule Lake camp in northeastern California.

Tule Lake became the "maximum-security segregation center" for these "disloyals" and their family members. Forty-two percent of its population had answered no to the loyalty questions or refused to register. There were also nearly three thousand "renunciants" at Tule Lake, people who, after the way they had been treated in America, had expressed a willingness to return to or go to Japan.

Michi hoped to "break new ground" by "thrusting deeper into the dark, hushed chapter that was Tule Lake," describing it as a "'resegregation center' for democracy's discards" with "a half-dozen tanks patrolling its outer perimeter and a guard contingent of campaign-equipped troops at full battalion strength."

"Had equally impressive preparations been made in the area of housing, sanitation, mess operation, health care, and other more human considerations, those forced to undergo another uprooting and resettlement might have been spared the debacle on debacle that followed," Michi argued. "But a situation ripe for upheaval was set up in the 'benign neglect'—or woeful miscalculation—which found over 18,000 segregants of widely divergent loyalties jammed into space meant for 15,000."

After a farm-truck accident killed one and seriously injured five in October 1943, the workers on Tule Lake's 2,900 acres of farm fields refused to return to work. Representatives demanded improvement of conditions in the camp, including relief from the overcrowding, better sanitation, more milk for the children and better food for all, that what was produced on the farm be consumed by those in the camp and not sold elsewhere, and that the administration accept responsibility for the accident. They also demanded that those at Tule Lake be treated as well as prisoners of war, and that the "loyals" and "fence-sitters" at the camp be physically separated from the "renunciants" who intended to relocate to Japan. When the camp administration responded by terminating the employment of some eight hundred of the farmworkers and bringing in strikebreakers—"loyal" laborers from the other WRA camps—the Tuleans increased their demands: reinstatement of all the terminated farmworkers, recognition of a self-governing body for the camp's residents, and the resignation of the camp director and other staff workers "harboring feelings of racial superiority," Michi wrote.

When WRA national director Dillon Myer visited Tule Lake on November 1, 1943, a crowd of over five thousand of the camp residents demonstrated to press their demands. Three days later, the army moved in, declaring martial law and swooping through the camp to find and arrest "anti-administration belligerents."

The "symbol of galling injustice" at Tule Lake, Michi wrote, was the "stockade"—a prison within the prison, six barrack buildings separated from the rest of the camp with their own barbed-wire fences and guard towers. The arrested leaders were taken there and detained for periods of one to nine months without any charges being filed. They were refused medical attention and any contact with family and friends, and beaten by guards. By the beginning of 1944, there were over 200 individuals in the stockade, and over 350 by April that year.

Michi called the U.S. government's version of events the "semantics of repression" when its officials replied that those sequestered in the stockade "had not even been arrested. They were merely undergoing 'administrative separation,'" she wrote.

For her reconstruction of events at the Tule Lake camp, Michi received immense help from two attorneys working for the American Civil Liberties Union, Ernest Besig and Wayne M. Collins.

In this 1944 photo, which Michi notes in Years of Infamy *was one of those "smuggled" out of Tule Lake by Wayne Collins, camp protesters are arrested.*

Besig, the wartime director of the Northern California ACLU, supplied Michi with affidavits (legal, sworn statements by individuals) taken during two days of interviews at Tule Lake in July 1944. Despite the objections and hostile reception from the camp administration, Besig learned of the presence of the "little stockade," in which detainees were forced to live in tents during the winter; meals consisting of about a spoonful of rice with a carrot on top; and the brutality of the Internal Security officers, the camp's civilian police, who in some instances beat their charges with baseball bats.

Each of the eight detainees whom Besig interviewed stated that "he had sought unsuccessfully to ascertain the grounds of his detention" and that camp administration officials, including the camp director, encouraged the detainees to renounce their American citizenship so they could be removed from the camp.

Besig also noted that, within the Tule Lake camp, the "loyals" and "disloyals" were mixed together, and that the "disloyals" were becoming increasingly pro-Japan, creating a potentially explosive situation.

At the time Besig took his affidavits, pro-Japan sentiments and activities were increasing in the camp, mostly advocated and led by the older Issei generation, who were prohibited from American citizenship, and younger Kibei, who had been educated in Japan. "Why stay where we're not wanted?" and "We have the chance of being equal for having the same colored skin" in Japan became increasingly prevalent attitudes. Classes teaching the Japanese language and the cultural ways of Japan were held. These activities became more militant and militaristic, with 6 a.m. calisthenics led by Kibei drillmasters and open displays of the

Members of the Hoshi Dan back-to-Japan movement demonstrate at Tule Lake.

Rising Sun on shirts, headbands, and flags. The back-to-Japan movement was dominated and directed by a group called the Sokuji Kikoku Hoshi Dan (Organization to Return Immediately to the Homeland to Serve) and its young, mostly Kibei supporters, the Hokoku.

The Nisei, who had lived all their lives in the United States, grew uneasy and concerned. How would what was going on at Tule Lake impact their future once the war ended? When the closure of all the War Relocation Authority camps holding Japanese Americans was announced in December 1944, those incarcerated at Tule Lake were left with an intimidating choice: Do they take their chances and strike out alone or with their families into a possibly hostile America with no guarantee of food, finances, and housing? Or, for those who were American citizens, do they renounce that citizenship and go to Japan?

The U.S. Justice Department started to process renunciations. The Hokoku and Hoshi Dan stepped up intimidation to renounce. Others faced indecision about a future in America. These events brought the camp into "a frenzy of renunciation hysteria," Michi wrote.

"The failure of camp authorities to institute protective measures in the interest of the large neutral majority ended up in a veritable reign of terror."

Willingly or via coercion, a total of 5,461 residents at Tule Lake filed to renounce their citizenship. "Seven out of every ten Nisei had taken the fatal step," Michi wrote. By comparison, from the other nine War Relocation camps, a combined total of 128 applied to be sent to Japan.

In 1944, Ernest Besig had sought the help of another ACLU attorney, Wayne Collins, in shutting down the stockade at the Tule Lake camp. Collins threatened WRA with making the existence of the stockade known to the public, and a lawsuit for denying the stockade prisoners the writ of habeas corpus—the reason why they were being imprisoned there. During August of that year, Collins visited Tule Lake to find the stockade dismantled. When Collins returned in July 1945 after learning that the stockade had been reactivated, parents of renunciants desperately sought him out for legal counsel. Unable to find other lawyers willing to help, he initially took on almost a thousand cases. He was warned not to represent those considered "dangerous to national security" and was shunned by other attorneys. His only supporters remained Ernest Besig and the Northern California ACLU chapter.

In the U.S. District Court, San Francisco, on November 13, 1945, Collins argued to prevent the Justice Department from proceeding with 987 renunciants' deportations, and to restore U.S. citizenship to each. He charged that the renunciations were a "fraud" and he placed

Attorney Wayne Collins, pictured with Iva Toguri, a Nisei woman who was tried for treason in the United States for serving as a Japanese propagandist during World War II (see page 124).

the onus on the U.S. government for allowing "a small pro-Japanese clique" to "force loyal Americans into repudiating their citizenship," Michi wrote. He also charged the U.S. government with failure to protect his clients from the Hokoku/Hoshi Dan and to invoke criminal laws against the group.

The court issued a "last-minute stay" and the lawyer "literally raced on board ships to remove clients," according to Michi.

Over the next fourteen years, Collins pursued through the courts the cases of people held at Tule Lake and other camps, at first halting 4,700 of them from being unwillingly deported to Japan. In 1959, the attorney general announced that a final review of the cases had been completed, and 4,978 of the Nisei renunciants had their citizenship restored.

"By this time," Michi wrote, "2,031 renunciants had gone to Japan. Of the 3,735 who remained in the United States, all but eighty-four had regained their citizenship."

Michi summarized, "Collins was to write and file some 10,000 affidavits in defense of, and in redefense of, his numerous clients, both in the United States and Japan." In an endnote, she added: "Wayne Collins passed away suddenly on July 16, 1974, yet he lives on in the memory of thousands who were the beneficiaries of his fierce dedication to justice."

Michi ended up dedicating her book to Wayne Collins: "Who Did More to Correct a Democracy's Mistake Than Any Other One Person."

chapter 12

The enormity of a bygone injustice has
been only partially perceived.
—Michi Nishiura Weglyn

THE U.S. GOVERNMENT CALLED WHAT

Michi had undergone as a teenager an "evacuation." The slapdash temporary housing in Turlock, ringed by barbed wire and armed guards, the government called an "assembly center." The camp at Gila River—a "relocation center."

When these "relocation centers" began to be more openly talked about during the time Michi was working on her book, they became known as "internment" camps. However, academics and historians later took issue with that term. It has always been legal under American law to "intern" aliens—those not American citizens—from countries with which the United States is at war. Therefore, it would be technically—legally—correct to identify the twenty-four camps operated by the U.S. Department of Justice and U.S. military that detained Issei community leaders and Japanese Latin Americans as "internment" camps. But what, then, to call the ten WRA camps that held the Nisei, American-born U.S. citizens?

A term that has been, and still is, controversial is "concentration camps"—debated since it makes comparisons to the death camps operated by the Nazis in Europe. No executions were carried out in the American World War II camps. Michi discovered that seven Japanese Americans were slain by U.S. sentries, including the two who died in the 1942 Manzanar riot. U.S. Army courts called these slayings "attempted escapes" and acquitted the sentries.

Michi found that members of the Roosevelt administration did use the term "concentration camps." In late 1944, after President Roosevelt had been elected to an unprecedented fourth term, he stated at a press conference, "It is felt by a great many lawyers that under the Constitution they can't be kept locked up in concentration camps."

In a newspaper interview after the war, in 1946, Interior Secretary Harold Ickes said, "We gave the fancy name of 'relocation centers' to these dust bowls, but they were concentration camps nonetheless."

It was Ickes, "the in-house critic of the whole sordid matter of 'fancy-named concentration camps'—as he called them," Michi wrote, who "had started the momentum for liberation. The pivot on which the evacuation had turned was 'military necessity.' Ickes was insisting that this was all nonsense now, that even the Army considered the argument unjustifiable."

"There are, of course, strong political reasons why the Japanese should not be returned to the West Coast before next November, but these do not concern the Army," wrote Army Chief of Staff Gen. George C. Marshall to Assistant War Secretary McCloy. Those "political reasons" included not losing votes in a presidential election by taking an unpopular action.

In December 1944 the U.S. Supreme Court ruled that a loyal citizen could no longer be detained. However, Michi noted that the Court "found it unnecessary" to address "the constitutional issues involved; and it chose not to find the 'big guns'—the military, the President, or Congress—culpable for what had been perpetrated in the intervening years."

She wrote: "The more fundamental gut concern of many, that the nearly three-year moral atrocity—the imprisonment, the physical and mental abuse, of thousands of men, women and children not accused of crime—violated and grotesquely distorted nearly every guarantee of the Bill of Rights, the Supreme Court carefully chose to sidestep."

Michi ended her book by updating what had happened to Japanese Americans up until the early 1970s—the time in which she was writing. While some thirty years before, the stereotype of her, her family, and her community members would have been of the sneaky, treacherous enemy, a new one had emerged—"America's model minority."

For Japanese Americans to get to that point—still a prevailing stereotype for Americans of Asian descent—Michi credited the "residual dignity" of her parents' generation, which "prevented disaster from becoming a catastrophe," by "continuing to stress patience, obedience, and duty more than rights. By demanding of one another the subordination of self to the larger interest. By urging in their children unstinting allegiance to their country—their 'master'—right or wrong.

"The innate moral fiber of the Issei, the resilience, their quiet poise under pressure, helped to soften the impact for the Nisei," she wrote.

However, "model minority" or not, as Michi pointed out, there was, and still is, an undeniable fact that remained for the Nisei and the generations after.

"Thirty years after being held accountable for what Japan had done, and paying an agonizingly high price for the right to be called Americans, the Japanese Americans realize that, like it or not, they are still looked upon as 'foreigners' in the land of their birth—linked inextricably with Japan."

It was the children of the Nisei who questioned their parents' and grandparents' dismissal of their treatment during World War II and afterward. The Sansei generation, she wrote, had proceeded to "dredge up" the past of "a whole generation clubbed into timidity and silence" while "the Nisei importuned: Let bygones be bygones. Why unnecessarily imperil their hard-won 'acceptance'? Why risk exposure to the often startling bigotry that lies below the façade of tolerance? Especially resented by the Nisei was their having to finally face up to the full extent of America's betrayal of their adolescent dreams and idealism.

"But after the initial pain of wounds reopened," Michi concluded, the "older generation began to recognize, however reluctantly, the merit of the Sansei's determination that the story be remembered, studied and talked about so that people will be forever reminded that concentration camps and wholesale contempt for individual rights and lawful procedure are not the exclusive province of corrupt tyrannies and maniacal dictatorships."

chapter 13

*For a long time we felt we were atoning
for the treachery of Pearl Harbor,
but the stain had to be eradicated.*
—Michi Nishiura Weglyn

THIRTY-FOUR YEARS TO THE DAY AFTER
President Roosevelt issued Executive Order 9066, which changed
Michi's and thousands of others' lives forever—President Gerald
R. Ford signed a proclamation titled "An American Promise," on
February 19, 1976. The decree officially rescinded Roosevelt's execu-
tive order. However, nowhere in the proclamation did it state that the
fault lay with the U.S. government.

For the title of her book, Michi decided on her own version of
President Roosevelt's words after the attack on Pearl Harbor: "a date
which will live in infamy." She called it *Years of Infamy: The Untold Story
of America's Concentration Camps.*

During her eight years of researching and writing, Michi sought an American company to publish her manuscript, which dared to challenge the history that had often been written—that what had happened to her was justified, or that it wasn't that difficult, or even that it had happened at all, as the subject was rarely covered in history books. Michi stuck to what she had. She had the proof. All the work she had done had to be worth it.

She sent her manuscript to publishers, who rejected it and replied that the content of her proposed book was "objectionable."

"Objectionable to whom?" Michi wanted to know.

Her husband Walter "forced me to persist in finishing *Years of Infamy* ... even when it became obvious that no publisher would touch the manuscript," Michi said. "He considered it my life mission and would not let me give up."

After rejections from a number of publishers, Michi found Howard Cady, an editor at William Morrow and Company, who believed in her book. It was finally released in 1976.

Years of Infamy: The Untold Story of America's Concentration Camps received national acclaim, especially from one of the most influential book reviewers, the *New York Times*, which described it as "fascinating and shattering ... extraordinary history." *Kirkus Reviews* assessed the book as "certainly the most documented account of WW II Japanese American internment."

Possibly more meaningful to Michi was praise from her peers who had written about and were authorities on her subject, and from the Japanese American community. Ohio State University sociologist Dr. William Petersen, an authority on the Japanese American mindset who

Years of Infamy is praised for its documentation of the "grim reality" of the World War II Japanese American experience.

assisted Michi in her research, stated, "The phrase in the subtitle, 'the untold story,' is not a publisher's blurb but the truth. It is a remarkable tribute to [Weglyn's] tenacity and intelligence that she has unearthed documents that a series of trained scholars and reporters overlooked."

Dr. Clifford Uyeda, JACL national president during that time, wrote in his blurb for Michi's book: "One of the most significant publications of this decade—not merely to Japanese Americans but to all Americans. This significance will be recognized more and more as the years go by."

However, as quoted in a newspaper story, Dr. Uyeda also noted that, due to Michi's blunt assessments and conclusions, there were bookstores that refused to display her book. In a later speech, Uyeda went on to say, "I recall the statement Michi made to me many years ago: 'When I wrote that book, I was hoping Nisei would become angry.' She had accomplished her purpose."

Years of Infamy provided an opening for Japanese Americans to begin talking about those dark years they had repressed. The stain of shame had been removed, Michi would later say. What happened to them during World War II was not because of anything they had done.

Michi's book also boosted the national "redress movement" by providing further proof of the U.S. government's actions during World War II.

In 1978 the JACL committed to creating a national legislative strategy to obtain redress through changes in the law. Other Japanese Americans formed organizations to pursue other means of obtaining redress. Formed in Seattle in 1979 and later Chicago based, the National Coalition for Japanese American Redress (NCJAR) pursued a class-action lawsuit (filed on behalf of a large group of people—in this case 125,000 victims) seeking compensation totaling $27.5 billion. Michi was a key supporter of the NCJAR approach.

In November 1979, Washington State representative Mike Lowry introduced the first redress bill into the U.S. Congress, seeking $15,000 each and $15 per diem (paid by the day; in this case, paid per day incarcerated) for those forcibly removed and detained. His bill proved unsuccessful. In 1980, California redress-advocacy groups formed the National Coalition for Redress/Reparations (NCRR) to educate the public through letter writing and rallies.

Urged by Hawaii senator Daniel Inouye, JACL campaigned for a federal investigation into the losses suffered by the Japanese Americans. President Jimmy Carter authorized the Commission on Wartime Relocation and Internment of Civilians, which held hearings in cities across the country from July through December 1981. It listened to three-minute testimonies of losses incurred—not only the loss of property but also the destruction of lives.

Michi testified at one of those hearings. The commission's report, which was to become the book *Personal Justice Denied*, concluded that there was misconduct and "grave injustices" committed on the part of the U.S. government. The commission wrote:

"The promulgation of Executive Order 9066 was not justified by military necessity, and the decisions which followed from it— detention, ending detention and ending exclusion—were not driven by analysis of military conditions. The broad historical causes which shaped these decisions were race prejudice, war hysteria and a failure of political leadership."

The commission recommended that the government issue a formal apology, that the survivors of the incarceration be issued $20,000 each, and that funding for education on the subject be established.

Based on the commission's recommendations, a series of bills was introduced in Congress, culminating in House Resolution (HR) 442—named in tribute to the Nisei 442nd Regimental Combat Team—introduced by Texas representative Jim Wright in January

Then a member of Congress, Norman Mineta shakes hands with President Ronald Reagan after the president signs the Civil Liberties Act of 1988. The legislation provides for a letter of apology and a $20,000 reparation check to those Japanese Americans who, like Michi, had been forced to leave their homes during World War II.

1985. A Senate version, introduced by Senator Spark Matsunaga of Hawaii, followed. That fall, JACL embarked on a nationwide letter-writing campaign and its representatives made personal visits to members of Congress, lobbying in support of the bill. Final redress bills were introduced in both houses of Congress in 1987.

During that same year, the NCJAR lawsuit reached the U.S. Supreme Court, which ruled against the case. The following year, the Court refused to hear NCJAR's second appeal of the suit, ending the effort.

In September 1987, the House passed HR 442, followed by the Senate in July 1988. Finally, on August 10, 1988, President Ronald Reagan signed into law the bill that became known as the Civil Liberties Act of 1988. Two years later, in October 1990, those who underwent forced removal and incarceration during World War II—and who were still alive when the act was signed—received their federal checks and a letter of apology from President George H. W. Bush.

Michi received her $20,000 check. She had been instrumental in the United States of America becoming one of the few nations in world history to admit a past error and apologize to its victims.

chapter 14

Do not sanctify ignorance by your silence.

—Michi Nishiura Weglyn

BUT MICHI DIDN'T STOP THERE. THERE
was still unfinished business. There were those who didn't receive the
letter of apology and payment, but should have . . .

In the course of conducting her research, she discovered events
that didn't make it into her book. One involved Japanese Americans
who lived and worked inland, away from the U.S. West Coast, on the
American railroads and mines.

Michi located a telegram from early February 1942, from FBI
director J. Edgar Hoover to W. M. Jeffers, president of the Union
Pacific Railroad. Hoover assured Jeffers that U.S. Attorney General
Francis Biddle would contact him about "the matter we discussed."
In a letter of February 11, 1942, from Union Pacific president Jeffers
to Col. W. T. Bals of U.S. Military Intelligence, Jeffers wrote that he

had talked with the FBI and Attorney General Biddle, and that "they saw no objection" to the firing of all of Union Pacific's workers of Japanese descent.

On February 13, Union Pacific fired 190 of those workers, and evicted them from company-owned homes, leaving them jobless and homeless. Other railroad companies did the same, firing a number of Japanese workers, estimated to total hundreds more. Union Pacific gave the Japanese Americans three days' notice; Southern Pacific allowed one day. They were dismissed without cause or explanation. Michi would say later:

"Considering that the orders involved workers who had served the line for decades, some of whom had just been warmly cited for their loyalty, only an agency of the government, such as the FBI or the military, could have ordered such cold-blooded action."

"In the camps, we were at least provided with food, medical attention, a roof, school and work," Michi said. "But the railroad workers had to roam around like homeless people in a hate-filled America. Their children are entitled to redress."

Michi also fought for Japanese American coal and copper miners, mostly laboring in the American West, who had been summarily fired.

Banging away on the same typewriter on which she wrote *Years of Infamy*, she wrote a flood of letters to the editors of newspapers and encouraged family members, the descendants of those Japanese American railroad workers and miners, to do the same. The Office of Redress Administration (ORA), the federal agency established to handle redress disbursements, was set to close in 1998. Michi wrote all the way to the top.

In a letter to President Bill Clinton she urged that the ORA consider "another ignored category of long-suffering applicants, the railroad and mine workers and others caught in ubiquitous 'military zones' established in areas surrounding plants, utilities, bridges, radio stations, etc. deemed strategic. Enough evidence has come up to prove the government's involvement in the layoffs of railroad and mine workers; and, worse, of entire families being evicted overnight from their domiciles, some of whom were subjected to shocking human rights violations by being made to live like cornered animals under armed guards, denied food, medical care, schooling, decent shelter and sanitary facilities."

Michi concluded: "I therefore share a special concern that the landmark redress program ends on a note of triumph, so that we may be able to celebrate with you in August, 1998 the greatness of a nation which responded justly to the cries of all of the once wronged, even 'the forgotten ones' ignored by history and by top historians. We must all apologize for this failure—to acknowledge those who have suffered the most."

Just making the deadline, President Clinton recognized the railroad and mine workers, and they received their apology letter and payments.

Japanese Latin Americans, particularly Peruvians, were "literally kidnapped" by the United States, Michi said. They were interned in the U.S. Justice Department camps at Kenedy, Seagoville, and Crystal City in Texas and at Santa Fe, New Mexico.

As Michi described: "Men were picked up off the streets or seized in their homes by the local police, then turned over to American authorities and shipped to U.S. concentration camps. It was an Orwellian nightmare, as all were first turned into 'illegal aliens' before landing on American soil by the confiscation of their papers and passports."

The Peruvian government "refused reentry of its unwanted ethnics" after the end of World War II, Michi continued. The U.S. State Department then declared that the Japanese Peruvians were "illegally" in the United States and proceeded to transport about 1,700 of them "voluntarily" to Japan. "Many had acquiesced to this drastic federal action in the belief that reunion with families left behind in Peru could not otherwise be achieved," Michi wrote.

However, 365 Japanese Peruvians still in the United States were not allowed to remain but, at the same time, were prohibited from returning to Peru. Again, attorney Wayne Collins interceded, appealing directly to the U.S. attorney general and the president (then Harry Truman, after the death of Franklin Roosevelt in 1945) to prevent their deportation. Ultimately, they were allowed to remain and, in 1952 with the McCarran-Walter immigration law, were able to become naturalized American citizens. However, these Japanese Latin Americans were denied redress. Michi said during a 1993 speech:

"I offer my conjecture that our Washington power brokers, still dominated by elitists with Eurocentric world vision (possibly disdainful of the lower two-thirds of the Americas), lack the empathy to put human faces on people whom America had once treated as no more than blocks of wood—just bodies to be bartered. They lack the depth of feeling to deal compassionately with our one-time hostages in a spirit of justice which the Civil Liberties Act of 1988 was meant to embody.

"For these are people who have few friends and advocates. And their votes don't count. As in the case of Native Americans. Native Hawaiians. Bikini Islanders. And so it goes."

In 1996, the former Japanese Latin Americans detained in America and their families formed the "Campaign for Justice." Over the next three years, it filed five lawsuits against the U.S. government to obtain redress payments. The government settled, agreeing to issue individual apology letters and to pay those detained during the war $5,000 each. Of the over 500 eligible, only 145 had received payments when the ORA ran out of funds. Efforts continue for Japanese Latin Americans to be granted the recognition and the $20,000 Japanese Americans received.

Michi was also an ardent advocate for another type of redress—for the Nisei draft resisters during World War II whom she described in *Years of Infamy* as "youths ending up in federal penitentiaries for taking a stand for the restoration of basic human rights before they would take up arms for a freedom that neither they nor their parents enjoyed."

In January 1944, the U.S. Selective Service began drafting Nisei out of the camps to serve in the U.S. armed forces. Out of those ordered to report for induction, 315 refused, arguing that they would not serve unless their rights—and their family members' rights—as Americans were restored. As opposed to "draft dodgers" who run away from being drafted, these young men were willing to accept the consequences for their stand.

Federal marshals whisked the draft resisters out of the camps and into local jails, near the federal courtrooms where they would stand trial. Convicted, they were then transported to federal penitentiaries, with most serving up to three years in prisons at Leavenworth, Kansas, and McNeil Island, Washington, and at the federal prison camp at Tucson, Arizona. Sixty-three were convicted together during a mass trial at the Cheyenne, Wyoming, federal court.

President Harry S. Truman pardoned all the Nisei draft resisters in 1947. But upon release, they were treated like pariahs by their fellow Japanese Americans; animosity between Nisei who served in the military and those who refused sometimes continued for the rest of their lives. JACL participated in the ostracism of the draft resisters.

Michi, seeking to clear the name of these resisters and arguing that theirs was an honorable cause, again embarked on a letter-writing campaign. Among those she wrote to was her former classmate from

Butte High School, Helen Kawagoe, a candidate for JACL national president in 1988. Michi wrote:

"I'm referring to the continuing hostility (poor choice of word?) between the draft resisters in camp and those who claim that only men who served their country deserve real recognition for accelerating our acceptance after the war. I would like to live to see some reconciliation—and recognition—to those who addressed the same principles in their unique and heroic way. Could it not be possible to effect something similar to the 'Welcome Home' for Vietnam veterans? Does JACL have such a poverty of spirit that they would

Sixty-three draft resisters from the Heart Mountain Relocation Center appear in court in Cheyenne, Wyoming, 1944.

be opposed to a public acknowledgment of the contribution of the resisters?"

In 2002, JACL delivered a national, formal apology to the draft resisters as "resisters of conscience."

Before then, at a 1998 Los Angeles event honoring Michi, Toshiko Kawamoto spoke about her husband, a 1942 NCAA wrestling champion at San Jose State College. Just weeks away from graduating, he and his family were ordered to the Pomona Assembly Center and

Michi gathers with former draft resisters and their supporters in Los Angeles in 1998. Seated, from left: Takashi Hoshizaki and James Kado. Standing, from left: Mits Koshiyama, Kenji Taguma, Noboru Taguma, Frank Emi, Michi, Yosh Kuromiya, and Toshiko Kawamoto.

then the Heart Mountain camp, where he became one of the sixty-three draft resisters. She went on to say:

"When Michi learned that Dave had not graduated in 1942 because of evacuation, she wrote to President Robert Caret at San Jose State University. After the faculty evaluation, I was notified that a posthumous Bachelor's degree would be awarded to Dave and I was asked to speak at the commencement exercises. Michi's letter must have been effective. I was overwhelmed. It was an honor to receive his diploma made possible by the concerted and kind efforts of Michi."

Mrs. Kawamoto concluded: "Through the years, Michi and Walter's friendship encouraged the resisters to return to their communities and stand up for what they did to set right the wrong done to all Japanese Americans. On behalf of my family, I want to express my most sincere appreciation to Michi for all she has done to benefit so many."

chapter 15

An innocent to an exhausted activist.

—Michi Nishiura Weglyn

FOR HER *YEARS OF INFAMY*, MICHI received the Japanese American Biennium Award from JACL at its 1976 national convention—from the organization whose policies, past and present, she challenged.

She received the Anisfield-Wolf Award in Race Relations for *Years of Infamy* in 1977, and the Justice in Action Award from the Asian American Legal Defense and Education Fund in 1987.

And for someone who didn't earn a college degree, Michi more than made up for it. She received an honorary degree of Doctor of Letters from Hunter College, New York, in 1992. In 1993, she was given her honorary Doctor of Humane Letters degree from California State University and an official proclamation by the City of New

York. That same year, California Polytechnic University in Pomona, California, established the Michi and Walter Weglyn Endowed Chair for Multicultural Studies. Funding for this program to bring in guest speakers and scholars to promote multiculturalism was begun by a donation from Michi and Walter. To this endowment, Michi then dedicated all future royalties from her book.

Michi finally, in a roundabout way, graduated from Mount Holyoke College in 1994, with an honorary degree of Doctor of Letters, and also received an honorary doctorate from Smith College, in Northampton, Massachusetts. The redress organization, the National Coalition for Redress/Reparations, awarded her the Fighting Spirit Award in 1998.

Michi is congratulated when she receives her honorary degree from Mount Holyoke College, 1994.

Michi also continuously fought for those whose fates had been apparently—but wrongly—sealed. She wrote her typical flood of letters to exonerate Iva Toguri, a Nisei stuck in Japan after the outbreak of World War II who was convicted in 1949 of treason for being "Tokyo Rose," a radio propagandist for the Japanese. She served six years in prison and had her U.S. citizenship revoked. "Only by a massive support for a speedy Presidential pardon, and a restoration of her citizenship, can we Americans demonstrate that democracy can—and does—correct its own mistakes," read one letter.

After coerced false testimony against her was revealed, President Gerald Ford pardoned Toguri in early 1977.

Michi did the same for Chol Soo Lee, a twenty-year-old immigrant from South Korea convicted for a 1973 shooting death in San Francisco, later also convicted for the stabbing of a fellow prison inmate. The national Korean American community—and then Asian Americans nationwide—came to Lee's defense, contending that he had been framed by unreliable witnesses and never committed the shooting, and had acted in self-defense during the stabbing. As she did for Iva Toguri, Michi helped mobilize national media coverage, and Lee was acquitted of both murders in 1983.

And then Michi advocated for a mass, anonymous group of "forgotten ones." In a 1983 letter to the editor of the *New York Times*, Michi wrote: "Could not restaurants in our city consider adopting a few families each—families who have been certified as in desperate financial straits—to become recipients of clean, carefully put aside

Michi (right) joins a 1993 protest in New York against the
film Rising Sun. The novel on which the film is based portrays
a fictitious Japanese takeover of American industry.

leftovers, which could be picked up on days mutually agreeable to the
parties involved? Yes, leftovers. . . .

"As a former dishwasher (after freedom gained from an Arizona-
based citizens detention camp during World War II) and a witness for
decades to the incredible waste tolerated on the 'outside,' I know
that a little resourcefulness could perform miracles in halting the
waste. And thousands now facing awful diseases and the cruelty of
slow, lingering deaths from hunger might possibly be saved."

In 1995, Walter was diagnosed with glioblastoma multiforme—
terminal brain cancer. Michi, herself in frail health from the lifelong

effects of tuberculosis, refused to accept the diagnosis. She and Walter searched for an alternative, trying natural "holistic" treatment in Mexico rather than the usual medical procedures in America.

On the eve of traveling to Mexico, Sachi Seko, a lifelong friend who Michi met at the Gila River camp, recalled: "His usually vibrant voice was barely audible, a labored whisper. 'I have to live to finish our work. We must secure redress for the families of railroad and mine workers and Latin American hostages,' he said. 'We must win.'"

Michi took Walter to Tijuana for treatment; he passed away in nearby San Diego in August 1995 at age sixty-nine. He had worked for forty-eight years at International Flavors and Fragrances, and been Michi's husband for forty-five.

In responding to letters of condolence, including those from the Netherlands, Michi wrote about Walter as "my true pillar of strength and the most important thing in my life, for he took a chronic invalid and breathed life, confidence and hope into one condemned. It was a veritable miracle, but it was that selflessness that characterized his life . . . his proclivity for philanthropy and in helping the downtrodden, whatever their skin color."

Three years later, in 1998, Michi was diagnosed with stomach cancer. Like Walter, she was an advocate for alternative medicine and opted for "psychic surgery" in the Philippines, recalled Sachi Seko. Sachi was opposed to the idea, but, as she remembered about Michi, "her tenacity served her well in intellectual pursuits, but often worked against her in practical matters." Experiencing temporary relief, her health began to deteriorate by year's end. "Death isn't bad," Michi had said. "It's getting there that's hell."

Convinced to receive traditional Western medicine, Michi was cared for by private nurses during her last two months, as her wish was to die at home in New York. She was "perfectly lucid to the end," recalled Sachi. "She never lost her intelligence or her quirky sense of humor." At age seventy-two, Michi Nishiura Weglyn passed away in her New York City apartment on April 25, 1999.

Michi is pictured with a photograph of Walter at her New York City apartment, about 1998.

Speaking of *Years of Infamy* and her mission since, Michi had said, "I have spoken with candor and forthrightness, telling it like it was. Its purpose—let me assure you—has been well intentioned, for it is my sincere hope that this story of what happened, only a generation ago, may serve as a sobering reminder to us all that even constitutions are not worth the parchment they are printed on, unless vitalized by a sound and uncorrupted public opinion and leadership of integrity and compassion."

Michi rocked the boat. She made waves.

To her, it had to be done.

She fought by using words, and only words.

And, Michi said: "By reading the life histories of individuals who have excelled in bettering the human condition, you will find their tragedies and triumphs to be a constant source of empowerment."

ACKNOWLEDGMENTS

My utmost appreciation to Jamie Henricks, archivist at the Japanese American National Museum; Sharon Yamato, co-filmmaker of *Out of Infamy: Michi Nishiura Weglyn*; Frank Abe, author and filmmaker of *Conscience and the Constitution*; Arnie Ohashi, who provided the rides in Los Angeles; agent Rosemary Stimola of Stimola Literary Studios, who initiated the process to publish this story; and Simon Boughton, publishing director of Norton Young Readers, who expressed early interest in this story and saw it through publication.

Chapter 1

1 ...... **"Until we extend":** Michi Nishiura Weglyn, "Text of Commencement Address Delivered at the College of Arts, California State Polytechnic University, Pomona, California, June 12, 1993," Michi Weglyn Collection, Japanese American National Museum (JANM), Los Angeles.

1 ...... **Michiko Nishiura grew up on a farm . . . water reached where she stood:** Shapiro, "Michi," 464–65; Kapitanoff and Yamato, *Out of Infamy*; Hong, *Notable Asian Americans*, 411–12.

3 ...... **Tomojiro Nishiura, Michiko's father . . . Tomiko came along:** Weglyn, "Biographical Data," Michi Weglyn Collection, JANM; Kapitanoff and Yamato, *Out of Infamy*.

5 ...... **As a girl . . . good impressions about her:** Shapiro, "Michi," 465–66; Hong, *Notable Asian Americans*, 411; Kapitanoff and Yamato, *Out of Infamy*; Christy, "So You Have a Figure Problem?"

6 ...... **"Michiko Nishiura of Excelsior School":** "The American Legion Certificate of School Award," June 10, 1940, Michi Weglyn Collection, JANM.

6 ...... **Together with . . . most popular student:** Shapiro, "Michi," 468–69.

Chapter 2

8 ...... **"This, under the circumstances":** Wegleyn, Michi Nishiura. Introduction by James A. Michener. *Years of Infamy: The Untold Story of America's Concentration Camps*, 21. Copyright 1996. This and subsequent quotations from this work reprinted with permission of the University of Washington Press.

9 ...... **Luckily, her teacher:** Shapiro, "Michi," 466.

10 ...... **Michiko and Tomiko awoke:** Ibid.

10 ...... **It authorized:** Weglyn, *Years of Infamy*, 69.

11 ...... **The date when the family:** Shapiro, "Michi," 466; General Services Administration, "Wartime Internment of Nishiura Family," November 1, 1978, Michi Weglyn Collection, JANM; McCarthy, "Exposed: America's World War II Concentration Camps."

12 ...... **One stranger proposed:** Shapiro, "Michi," 467.

13 ...... **U.S. Army soldiers . . . for Japanese Americans:** Burton et al., *Confinement and Ethnicity*, 377–78; Brian Niiya, "Turlock (Detention Facility)," Densho Encyclopedia, last revised December 30, retrieved on November 10, 2021, from 2020, https://encyclopedia.densho.org/Turlock_%28detention_facility%29/.

14 ...... **Used to her wide-open farm . . . filled with straw:** Shapiro, "Michi," 467; Angelina Martin, "75 Years Later: A Look Back at the Turlock Assembly Center," *Turlock Journal*, February 17, 2017, https://www.turlockjournal.com/news/local/75-years-later-a-look-back-at-the-turlock-assembly-center/.

14 ...... **Some exploded in outrage . . . would the war go on?:** Stone, *Peace Is a Chain Reaction*, 50; Commission on Wartime Relocation and Internment of Civilians, *Personal Justice Denied*, 135–48; Weglyn, Years of Infamy, 21.

Chapter 3

16 ...... **"I despise deserts":** Shapiro, "Michi," 470.

16 ...... **After over three months:** Shapiro, "Michi," 467–68.

16 ...... **Finally, they arrived . . . and mouths:** Shapiro, "Michi," 468; Burton et al., *Confinement and Ethnicity*, 59–61; Kapitanoff and Yamato, *Out of Infamy*.

20 ...... **Skilled professionals . . . made $12:** Commission on Wartime Relocation and Internment of Civilians, *Personal Justice Denied*, 166.

20 ...... **Tomojiro became sick:** Shapiro, "Michi," 468; "What Is Valley Fever?," WebMD, medically reviewed May 10, 2021, https://www.webmd.com/a-to-z-guides/valley -fever#1.

21 ...... **school was held:** Burton et al., *Confinement and Ethnicity*, 66–67.

21 ...... **She began to speak out:** Shapiro, "Michi," 468–69.

21 ...... **pay for their uniforms:** Ibid.; Michi Weglyn to Frank Chin, n.d., Densho Digital Repository/CSU Japanese American History Digitization Project, https://ddr .densho.org/media/ddr-csujad-24/ddr-csujad-24-90-mezzanine-e404587734.pdf.

23 ...... **Eleanor Roosevelt wrote an essay . . . "coddling" ever addressed:** Burton et al., *Confinement and Ethnicity*, 19–24; "Eleanor Roosevelt Papers, Speech and Article File, 1943," Franklin D. Roosevelt Presidential Library & Museum; Mrs. Franklin D. Roosevelt, "A Challenge to American Sportsmanship," *Collier's*, October 16, 1943.

Chapter 4

25 ...... **"At Gila, I was trying":** Shapiro, "Michi," 469.

25 ...... **"We hope by means":** "High Schools of Arizona to Participate in Events," *Girls' League Gazette*, Butte High School, April 15, 1944, Michi Weglyn Collection, JANM.

27 ...... **"Discussions were conducted":** "12 Schools Represented in State Confab Held at Butte," *Gila News-Courier*, April 8, 1942, Michi Weglyn Collection, JANM.

28 ...... **Despite her fear:** Ruth E. Thompson, "Michi Weglyn, Ex-Como Show Designer, Now an Author," *Eldorado Daily Journal*, July 30, 1976, Michi Weglyn Collection, JANM.

29 ...... **"With poise":** "Nishiura, Yamamoto Winners in Colony-Wide Oratorical," *Gila News-Courier*, 1944, Michi Weglyn Collection, JANM.

29 ...... **Around that same time:** "Three Students Named Winners," *Gila News-Courier*, 1944, Michi Weglyn Collection, JANM.

29 ...... **"There can be no . . . toward men":** "For Interracial Tolerance," Commission on World Peace, April 4, 1944, Michi Weglyn Collection, JANM.

30 ...... **"for having contributed":** "1943–1944, Certificate of Award, Butte High School, Rivers, Arizona," Michi Weglyn Collection, JANM.

30 ...... **"the most outstanding girl":** "Butte Scholar Awarded $1,100 Offer to College," *Gila News-Courier*, 1944, Michi Weglyn Collection, JANM.

30 ...... **"those high qualities":** "The American Legion Certificate of School Award," June 8, 1944, Michi Weglyn Collection, JANM.

30 ...... **An organization called:** Mochizuki, *Minidoka Memoirs: The Untold Story from the Yoshito Fujii Files*, 110–11.

31 ...... **a lengthy, dense epic:** "Evangeline," Wikipedia, accessed November 10, 2021, https://en.wikipedia.org/wiki/Evangeline.

31 ...... **"From the very first day":** "Year's Flight 1944," Butte High School, Gila River War Relocation Center, Rivers, Arizona, Michi Weglyn Collection, JANM.

32 ...... **"Go where no one else":** "History," Mount Holyoke, accessed November 10, 2021, https://www.mtholyoke.edu/about/history.

32 ...... **was refused service:** Shapiro, "Michi," 470.

32 ...... **"tuition and fees plus $260":** "Butte Scholar Awarded $1,100 Offer to College," *Gila News-Courier*, 1944, Michi Weglyn Collection, JANM.

34 ...... **A scary thought:** Shapiro, "Michi," 470.

Chapter 5

35 ...... **"From that moment on":** "Michi, Como's Costume Creator," *Kraft Cameraman*, 1962, Michi Weglyn Collection, JANM.

35 ...... **"big sister":** Thompson, "Michi Weglyn, Ex-Como Show Designer."

35 ...... **"They were as dear to me":** Ibid.

35 ...... **One of her professors:** Josephine Sakurai, "Evolution: Biology to Stage Costume Design," *Hokubei Shimpo*, April 2, 1953, Michi Weglyn Collection, JANM.

36 ...... **"The forest set":** Frances Unger, "D.C. Review," Michi Weglyn Collection, JANM.

36 ...... **"continued applause":** "She Joins Chol Soo Battle, Is Convinced He's Innocent," *The Joong-ang Daily News*, April 11, 1981, Michi Weglyn Collection, JANM.

36 ...... **would close the following year:** Mochizuki, *Minidoka Memoirs*, 158–59.

36 ...... **the most decorated:** Asahina, *Just Americans*, 5.

37 ...... **a case for the U.S. Supreme Court . . . to the U.S. West Coast:** Stephanie Buck, "Overlooked No More: Mitsuye Endo, a Name Linked to Justice for Japanese-Americans," *New York Times*, October 9, 2019, https://www.nytimes.com/2019/10/09/obituaries/mitsuye-endo-overlooked.html.

38 ...... **a disease dreaded . . . sanatorium:** "Tuberculosis (TB)," WebMD, medically reviewed June 27, 2020, https://www.webmd.com/lung/understanding-tuberculosis-basics#1; Mochizuki, *Meet Me at Higo: An Enduring Story of a Japanese American Family*, 33.

38 ...... **Michiko had been forced:** "She Joins Chol Soo Battle."

38 ...... **The company recruited . . . company grounds:** Kelli Nakamura, "Seabrook Farms," Densho Encyclopedia, last revised June 10, 2020, retrieved on November

10, 2021, from https://encyclopedia.densho.org/Seabrook_Farms/; Weglyn, *Years of Infamy*, 65.

39 ...... **Over eight hundred Japanese Americans ... than outside:** Higashide, *Adios to Tears*, 179–92.

40 ...... **Men were paid ... "Prisoner of Love":** John Seabrook, "The Spinach King," http://www.johnseabrook.com/the-spinach-king; Higashide, *Adios to Tears*, 182; "Michi Nishiura Visiting Glen Gardner Sanatorium," RUcore Rutgers University Community Repository, Rutgers University Libraries, https.//rucore.libraries .rutgers.edu/rutgers-lib/10151/record/; Kapitanoff and Yamato, *Out of Infamy*.

Chapter 6

41 ...... **"He turned a chronically ill":** Michi Weglyn to "Hein," December 1995, "Correspondence—Condolence," Resi Weglein Collection, AR 25633, Box 2, Folder 1. Courtesy of the Leo Baeck Institute, New York.

41 ...... **Michiko narrowed her focus:** "She Joins Chol Soo Battle."

42 ...... **Begun in 1924 ... from other countries:** "Our History," International House, https://www.ihouse-nyc.org/about-student-housing-in-ny/our-history/.

42 ...... **Walter grew up ... the war wounded:** "Biographical Note," Guide to the Papers of Resi Weglein, 1894–2007, AR 25633. Courtesy of the Leo Baeck Institute, New York, https://digifindingaids.cjh.org/?pID=2994177; Sidney Fields, "Only Human," *Daily News*, July 22, 1976, Michi Weglyn Collection, JANM.

42 ...... **Approximately ninety-two thousand Jews:** Morse, *While Six Million Died*, 105.

42 ...... **Walter was born:** "Biographical Note."

42 ...... **By 1933 ... businesses and synagogues:** Morse, *While Six Million Died*, 222–28.

43 ...... **That Siegmund Weglein:** Fields, "Only Human"; "Biographical Note."

43 ...... **Kindertransport:** Ernest Goodman and Melissa Hacker, "Kindertransport, European History [1938–1940]," Encyclopedia Britannica, accessed November 10, 2021, https://www.britannica.com/event/Kindertransport.

43 ...... **twelve-year-old Walter:** Fields, "Only Human."

44 ...... **He then found himself fortunate:** Kapitanoff and Yamato, *Out of Infamy*.

44 ...... **Among those assisting:** "Cal Poly Pomona Pays Its Respects to Walter M. Weglyn, Humanitarian and University Supporter," Cal Poly Pomona bulletin, September 5, 1995; "Correspondence—Condolence," Resi Weglein Collection, AR 25633, Box 2, Folder 1. Courtesy of the Leo Baeck Institute, New York.

44 ...... **There, the Nazis .. Red Army in 1945:** "Children's Drawings from Terezin," U.S. Holocaust Memorial Museum, Resi Weglein Collection, AR 25633, Box 3, Folder 8. Courtesy of the Leo Baeck Institute, New York.

44 ...... **he was to find out:** Chaplain (Capt.) Herbert S. Eskin to Fritz Rhea, relative of Walter Weglyn, June 25, 1945, Resi Weglein Collection, AR 25633, Box 2, Folder 2. Courtesy of the Leo Baeck Institute, New York.

45 ...... **he was one of only two:** Paul Tsuneishi and Frank Chin, "Michi Weglyn's Husband, Walter, Dies," *Rafu Shimpo*, August 24, 1995.

45 ...... **The friend introduced:** Michi Weglyn to "Loet and Marriane," September 29, 1995, "Correspondence—Condolence," Resi Weglein Collection, AR 25633, Box 2, Folder 1. Courtesy of the Leo Baeck Institute, New York.

45 ...... **He eventually went to work:** "Certificate of Death," August 28, 1995, and "Certificate of Naturalization," November 27, 1950, Resi Weglein Collection, AR 25633, Box 1, Folder 4. Courtesy of the Leo Baeck Institute, New York.

46 ...... **Walter visited:** "Cal Poly Pomona Pays Its Respects."

46 ...... **After leaving Seabrook Farms:** Sharon Yamato, email correspondence to author, November 29, 2021.

46 ...... **Both the Weglyn and Nishiura parents:** Kellar Ellsworth, "Interracial Marriage Was Actually Illegal in 16 States in 1967 (Loving v. Virginia)," Groovy History, https://groovyhistory.com/interracial-marriage-illegal-loving-v-virginia.

47 ...... **Michiko's mother was firmly against . . . they had experienced:** Kapitanoff and Yamato, *Out of Infamy*.

Chapter 7

48 ...... **"Glamour is an illusion":** Christy, "So You Have a Figure Problem," *TV Guide*, November 11, 1961. Copyrighted 1961. TVGM Holdings.

48 ...... **Other Japanese Americans . . . to the markets:** Brian Niiya, "Return to West Coast," Densho Encyclopedia, last revised October 8, 2020, retrieved November 9, 2021, from https://encyclopedia.densho.org/Return_to_West_Coast/#Return_to_Rural_Communities; "Brooks Andrews Interview," by Joyce Nishimura, October 7, 2006, Densho Digital Archives/Bainbridge Island Japanese American Community Collection, retrieved November 9, 2021, from https://ddr.densho.org/interviews/ddr-densho-1001-7-1/.

49 ...... **Those fortunate:** Niiya, "Return to West Coast."

49 ...... **were refused membership:** Del Rosario, "Richard H. Naito," in *A Different Battle*, 83; Linda Tamura, "Hood River Incident," Densho Encyclopedia, last revised June 9, 2020, retrieved November 10, 2021, from https://encyclopedia.densho.org/Hood_River_incident/; Calisphere, "Installation of Officers of the Sacramento Nisei VFW Post No. 8985," Japanese American Archival Collection, California State University, Sacramento Library, https://calisphere.org/item/ark:/13030/kt3r29q2w6/.

49 ...... **tried hard to be accepted:** Weglyn, *Years of Infamy*, 266–81.

50 ...... **was renovated in 1952:** "Roxy Theatre (New York City)," Wikipedia, last edited September 16, 2021, https://en.wikipedia.org/wiki/Roxy_Theatre_(New_York_City); "Roxy Theatre," Cinema Treasures, accessed November 10, 2021, http://cinematreasures.org/theaters/556.

50 ...... **"I like your work":** Sakurai, "Evolution: Biology to Stage Costume Design"; "'Michi' New Star of Stage Design," *New York Journal-American*, December 6, 1952, Michi Weglyn Collection, JANM.

50 ...... **"Wonderful. You're on your way"**: Sakurai, "Evolution"; "'Michi' New Star of Stage Design."

52 ...... **more *Ice Colorama* shows**: Sakurai, "Evolution."

52 ...... **"I realized then"**: Christy, "So You Have a Figure Problem?" Copyrighted 1961. TVGM Holdings.

52 ...... **and for *Skating Vanities***: Weglyn, "Biographical Data," Michi Weglyn Collection, JANM; "Gloria Nord," Wikipedia, last edited November 8, 2021, https://en .wikipedia.org/wiki/Gloria_Nord.

52 ...... **She kept a little black book**: Eloise Lang, "Resourceful Is Word for Como Designer," *St. Louis Post-Dispatch*, February 5, 1965, Michi Weglyn Collection, JANM. .

53 ...... **An anthology TV series**: "Kraft Television Theatre," Wikipedia, last edited November 1, 2021, https://en.wikipedia.org/wiki/Kraft_Television_Theatre.

54 ...... **"tendency to shorten"**: Christy, "So You Have a Figure Problem?" Copyrighted 1961. TVGM Holdings.

55 ...... **"everything from ferns to feathers"**: Ibid.

55 ...... **She spent hours researching**: Lang, "Resourceful Is Word."

55 ...... **costuming for some of the**: Weglyn, "Biographical Data."

55 ...... **Como's over-fifty-year career**: "Perry Como Television and Radio Shows," Wikipedia, last edited August 16, 2021, http://en.wikipedia.org/wiki/Perry_Como_ television_and_radio_shows.

55 ..... **In 1956, Michi began working**: Weglyn, "Biographical Data."

56 ...... **"The thing I strive for"**: Christy, "So You Have a Figure Problem?" Copyrighted 1961. TVGM Holdings.

56 ...... **Michi designed the wardrobes for**: Ibid.; Kapitanoff and Yamato, *Out of Infamy*.

57 ...... **"Don't you think that it's a testimonial"**: Christy, "So You Have a Figure Problem?" Copyrighted 1961. TVGM Holdings.

57 ...... **"a small, fragile beauty . . . Japanese-American Michi"**: Fields, "Only Human," courtesy *New York Daily News*; "'Michi' New Star of Stage Design."

57 ...... **"Leave her alone"**: Thompson, "Michi Weglyn, Ex-Como Show Designer."

Chapter 8

58 ...... **"From an apolitical innocent"**: Weglyn, "Commencement Address . . . California State Polytechnic."

58 ...... **were finally allowed**: Weglyn, *Years of Infamy*, 268.

58 ...... **Alien Land Laws**: "Alien Land Laws," Encyclopedia of Race and Racism, Ency- clopedia.com, October 26, 2021, https://www.encyclopedia.com/social-sciences/ encyclopedias-almanacs-transcripts-and-maps/alien-land-laws.

60 ...... **"Don't make waves!"**: Weglyn, *Years of Infamy*, 128, 266–81.

60 ...... **As Michi continued . . . with actor Robert Morse**: Weglyn, "Biographical Data."

61 ...... **"when the use of technological savagery"**: Weglyn, "Commencement Address . . . California State Polytechnic."

62 ...... **"the transition that took place"**: Ibid.

63 ...... **"southern and eastern Europeans were racially inferior":** From *While Six Million Died* by Arthur D. Morse. Copyright © 1967, 1968 by Arthur D. Morse. Used by permission of Abrams Press, an imprint of ABRAMS, New York. All rights reserved, 133.

63 ...... **The Immigration Act of 1924 ... England and Ireland:** Ibid., 134.

63 ...... **"had been directed at":** Ibid., 41.

63 ...... **remained indifferent:** Ibid., 107–29.

63 ...... **such as sports:** Ibid., 172–86.

64 ...... **"Failure to protest":** Ibid., 129.

64 ...... **"nullification or evasion":** Ibid., 62.

64 ...... **The Roosevelt administration ... "our Jewish citizens":** Ibid., 41–54, 62.

64 ...... **"Since he was afraid":** Ibid., 41.

64 ...... **"appalling apathy":** Kapitanoff and Yamato, *Out of Infamy*.

65 ...... **"We never have had":** *Meet the Press*, April 7, 1968, "Clark Ramsey statement not on Shaw—Hood College," Disk/Clark Ramsey Statement Not On Shaw/Item 01.pdf.; Kapitanoff and Yamato, *Out of Infamy*.

65 ...... **"startled me into disbelief":** Weglyn, "Commencement Address ... California State Polytechnic."

66 ...... **He talked with Michi:** Tsuneishi and Chin, "Michi Weglyn's Husband."

66 ...... **Michi recalled:** Kapitanoff and Yamato, *Out of Infamy*.

66 ...... **"I knew I was more":** Sachi Seko, "Digging for Roots," *Pacific Citizen*, February 27, 1976, www.pacificcitizen.org.

Chapter 9

67 ...... **"For an untrained researcher":** Weglyn, "Commencement Address ... California State Polytechnic."

67 ...... **New York Public Library:** McCarthy, "Exposed."

68 ...... **seventeen million pages:** "Historic Collections/Archives," Franklin D. Roosevelt Presidential Library and Museum, https://www.fdrlibrary.org/.

68 ...... **a report buried:** Weglyn, *Years of Infamy*, 34.

68 ...... **During October and November:** Ibid.

68 ...... **"considerably weakened in their loyalty ... treated as a foreigner":** Ibid., 41–44.

69 ...... **"There are still Japanese":** Ibid., 43.

69 ...... **"After interview after interview":** Ibid., 45–46.

70 ...... **"For the most part the local Japanese":** Ibid., 47.

70 ...... **"The consensus of opinion":** Ibid.

70 ...... **"with the full cooperation":** Ibid., 40.

70 ...... **"based primarily" ... the entire group:** Ibid., 35, 284.

71 ...... **"Your reporter, fully believing ... basis of equality":** Ibid., 51.

71 ...... **She made regular train trips . . . until the archives closed:** Phil Tajitsu Nash, "Michi Weglyn, Rosa Parks of the Japanese American Redress Movement, Dies at 72," Conscience and the Constitution, Resisters.com, April 26, 1999, https://www.resisters.com/htdocs/news/Michi_obit.htm.

73 ...... **"the hysteria":** Weglyn, "Commencement Address . . . California State Polytechnic."

73 ...... **trips out west:** McCarthy, "Exposed."

73 ...... **"Many Japanese Americans have been quiet":** Shapiro, "Michi," 464.

75 ...... **"non-conforming progressive":** Brian Niiya, "Emergency Detention Act, Title II of the Internal Security Act of 1950," Densho Encyclopedia, last revised July 15, 2020, retrieved on November 8, 2021, from https://encyclopedia.densho .org/Emergency_Detention_Act%2C_Title_II_of_the_Internal_Security_Act_ of_1950/; Alice Yang, "Edison Uno," Densho Encyclopedia, last revised June 24, 2020, retrieved on November 8, 2021, from https://encyclopedia.densho.org/ Edison_Uno/.

75 ...... **Under its proposal:** Weglyn, *Years of Infamy*, 281.

Chapter 10

76 ...... **"My God":** McCarthy, "Exposed."

76 ...... **"Evidence would indicate . . . for evacuation":** Weglyn, *Years of Infamy*, 34–35.

77 ...... **"Since much of Munson's documentation":** Ibid., 54.

77 ...... **"Continue our efforts . . . in the nation's capital":** Ibid., 62–63.

79 ...... **The Japanese Latin Americans:** Ibid., 59.

79 ...... **"would welcome their removal":** Ibid., 68.

80 ...... **The order would require:** Ibid., 67–72.

80 ...... **"never intended":** Ibid., 291.

80 ...... **The U.S. Congress:** Ibid., 72.

80 ...... **"Clearly, the lofty judiciary":** Ibid., 75.

82 ...... **"Repression was applied . . . must go to camp":** Ibid., 76–77.

83 ...... **"discouraging the called-for transplantation":** Ibid., 86–88.

83 ...... **To save the farm crops:** Ibid., 97–99.

84 ...... **"But had it not been for . . . without a hitch":** Ibid., 111–13.

84 ...... **"Native-born Japanese":** Ibid., 117.

86 ...... **"suffering from a chronic illness . . . only consolation left":** Ibid., 121–28.

86 ...... **"Walter is my most exacting critic":** Nash, "Michi Weglyn, Rosa Parks."

Chapter 11

87 ...... **"What I wanted":** "Michi Weglyn Interview," interview by Abe, Densho Digital Repository, Frank Abe Collection, retrieved on November 29, 2021, from https:// ddr.densho.org/narrators/164/.

87 ...... **"Ignoring the hurts ... to the United States"**: Weglyn, *Years of Infamy*, 135.

91 ...... **"The colossal folly"**: Ibid.

92 ...... **"Why the oath-taking now"**: Ibid., 145.

92 ...... **"proving irksome"**: Ibid.

92 ...... **Tule Lake became ... go to Japan**: Ibid., 154.

93 ...... **"thrusting deeper into the dark ... meant for 15,000"**: Ibid., 156–57.

93 ...... **After a farm-truck accident ... by April that year**: Ibid., 158–69, 204–5, 209; "Campu Episode Six: Food," Densho, retrieved on November 29, 2021, from https://densho.org/campu/campu-food/.

94 ...... **"had not even been arrested"**: Weglyn, *Years of Infamy*, 208.

96 ...... **Besig, the wartime director ... a potentially explosive situation**: Ibid., 208–14.

96 ...... **"Why stay where we're not wanted?"**: Ibid., 230–40.

98 ...... **"Seven out of every ten"**: Ibid., 247.

98 ...... **Collins threatened WRA ... "literally raced on board ships"**: Ibid., 253–56.

100 ...... **"Collins pursued through the courts ... both in the United States and Japan"**: Ibid., 256–65.

100 ...... **"Wayne Collins passed away"**: Ibid., 322.

100 ...... **"Who Did More to Correct a Democracy's Mistake"**: Ibid., 4.

Chapter 12

101 ...... **"The enormity of a bygone injustice"**: Nash, "Michi Weglyn, Rosa Parks."

102 ...... **Michi discovered that seven**: Weglyn, *Years of Infamy*, 312.

102 ...... **did use the term "concentration camps"**: Ibid., 175.

102 ...... **"It is felt by a great many lawyers"**: Ibid., 217.

102 ...... **"We gave the fancy name"**: Ibid., 316.

102 ...... **"the in-house critic ... considered the argument unjustifiable"**: Ibid., 218–20.

103 ...... **"There are, of course, strong political reasons"**: Ibid., 221.

103 ...... **"found it unnecessary ... chose to sidestep"**: Ibid., 228.

104 ...... **Michi credited the "residual dignity ... and maniacal dictatorships"**: Ibid., 266–81.

Chapter 13

106 ...... **"For a long time we felt"**: Fields, "Only Human," courtesy *New York Daily News*.

106 ...... **nowhere in the proclamation**: "Termination of Executive Order 9066," Densho Encyclopedia, last revised July 7, 2020, retrieved on November 9, 2012, from https://encyclopedia.densho.org/Termination_of_Executive_Order_9066/.

107 ...... **"Objectionable to whom?"**: Sachi Seko, "New York's Nominee," *Pacific Citizen*, July 9, 1976, www.pacificcitizen.org.

107 ...... **"forced me to persist":** Tsuneishi and Chin, "Michi Weglyn's Husband."

108 ...... **bookstores that refused:** Annie Nakao, "Michi Weglyn, champion of U.S. internees," *SFGate*, April 28, 1999, Michi Weglyn (sfgate.com).

109 ...... **"I recall the statement":** Kapitanoff and Yamato, *Out of Infamy.*

109 ...... **pursued a class-action lawsuit:** Weglyn, *Years of Infamy*, 282.

109 ...... **Michi was a key supporter:** Nash, "Michi Weglyn, Rosa Parks."

110 ...... **President Jimmy Carter ... destruction of lives:** Weglyn, Years of Infamy, 281–82; John Tateishi, "An Afternoon With The Author," Nisei Veterans Memorial Center, Maui, Hawaii, April 20, 2021, https://www .youtube.com/watch?v=cDXOh0FBoCl&t=2137s.

110 ...... **"The promulgation of Executive Order 9066":** Commission on Wartime Relocation and Internment of Civilians, *Personal Justice Denied*, 18.

110 ...... **The commission recommended ... President George H. W. Bush:** Weglyn, *Years of Infamy*, 281–82.

112 ...... **Michi received her $20,000 check:** Kapitanoff and Yamato, *Out of Infamy.*

Chapter 14

113 ...... **"Do not sanctify":** Weglyn, "Commencement Address ... California State Polytechnic."

113 ...... **Michi located ... without cause or explanation:** McCarthy, "Exposed."

114 ...... **"Considering that the orders":** Michi Weglyn speech at "Day of Remembrance," Los Angeles, February 21, 1998, Michi Weglyn Collection, JANM.

114 ...... **"In the camps, we were at least provided":** McCarthy, "Exposed."

115 ...... **"another ignored category ... those who have suffered the most":** Michi Weglyn, "Letter to the Editor: An Open Letter to President Clinton," *Nichi Bei Times*, November 5, 1997 (under "Letter from K.W. Lee to Friends of Michi Weglyn, November 1, 1997"), Densho Digital Repository/CSU Japanese American History Digitization Project, https://ddr.densho.org/media/ddr-csujad-24/ddr-csu-jad-24–203-mezzanine-20d1db1c7f.pdf.

116 ...... **"Men were picked up ... could not otherwise be achieved":** Weglyn, *Years of Infamy*, 64.

116 ...... **Ultimately, they were allowed:** Ibid., 64–66.

117 ...... **"I offer my conjecture ... And so it goes":** Weglyn, "Commencement Address ... California State Polytechnic."

117 ...... **In 1996, the former Japanese ... Japanese Americans received:** Stephen Mak, "Japanese Latin Americans," Densho Encyclopedia, last revised April 18, 2017, retrieved on November 12, 2021, from https://encyclopedia.densho.org/ Japanese_Latin_Americans/; Alice Yang, "Redress Movement," Densho Encyclopedia, last revised August 24, 2020, retrieved on November 12, 2021, from https:// encyclopedia.densho.org/Redress_movement/.

118 ...... **"youths ending up":** Weglyn, *Years of Infamy*, 126–27.

118 ...... **President Harry S. Truman pardoned:** Eric Muller, "Draft Resistance," Densho Encyclopedia, last revised August 24, 2020, retrieved on November 12, 2021, from https://encyclopedia.densho.org/Draft%20resistance/.

119 ...... **"I'm referring to ... contribution of the resisters?":** Michi Weglyn to Helen Kawagoe, June 14, 1988, Densho Digital Repository/CSU Japanese American History Digitization Project, http://ddr.densho.org/ddr-csujad-24–168/.

120 ...... **"resisters of conscience":** Cherstin M. Lyon, "JACL apology to draft resisters," Densho Encyclopedia, last revised August 24, 2020, retrieved on November 12, 2021, from https:/encyclopedia.densho.org/JACL%20apology/.

121 ...... **"When Michi learned ... to benefit so many":** Tribute to Michi Weglyn by Toshiko Kawamoto, February 21, 1998, Densho Digital Repository/CSU Japanese American History Digitization Project, https://ddr.densho.org/ddr-csujad-24-168/.

Chapter 15

122 ...... **"An innocent":** McCarthy, "Exposed."

122 ...... **the Japanese American Biennium Award ... the Fighting Spirit Award in 1998:** Hong, *Notable Asian Americans*.

124 ...... **"Only by a massive support ... correct its own mistakes":** Michi Weglyn, "A Pardon for 'Tokyo Rose,'" *New York Times*, November 22, 1976.

124 ..... **Michi did the same ... acquitted of both murders in 1983:** "She Joins Chol Soo Battle."

124 ...... **"Could not restaurants ... might possibly be saved":** Michi Weglyn, "What Restaurants Shouldn't Throw Away," *New York Times*, March 21, 1983.

126 ...... **"I have to live to finish":** Sachi Seko, "Remembering Walter Weglyn's Role in Redress," *Nichi Bei Times*, June 5, 1998; "Correspondence—Condolence," Resi Weglein Collection, AR 25633, Box 2, Folder 1. Courtesy of the Leo Baeck Institute, New York.

126 ...... **"my true pillar of strength":** Michi Weglyn to "Yohan and Stella," September 1995, "Correspondence—Condolence," Resi Weglein Collection, AR 25633, Box 2, Folder 1. Courtesy of the Leo Baeck Institute, New York.

127 ...... **"perfectly lucid to the end":** Sachi Seko, "Vox Populi: Remembering Michi Weglyn," *Rafu Shimpo*, April 28, 1999.

128 ...... **"I have spoken with candor":** Kapitanoff and Yamato, *Out of Infamy*.

128 ...... **"By reading the life histories":** Hong, *Notable Asian Americans*.

Asahina, Robert. *Just Americans: How Japanese Americans Won a War at Home and Abroad.* New York: Gotham Books, 2006.

Burton, Jeffery F., Mary M. Farrell, Florence B. Lord, and Richard W. Lord. *Confinement and Ethnicity: An Overview of World War II Japanese American Relocation Sites.* Tucson, AZ: Western Archeological and Conservation Center, 1999.

California State University Japanese American History Digitization Project. https://csujad.com.

Christy, George. "So You Have a Figure Problem?" *TV Guide*, November 11, 1961. Copyrighted 1961. TVGM Holdings.

Commission on Wartime Relocation and Internment of Civilians. *Personal Justice Denied.* Seattle: University of Washington Press, 1997.

Del Rosario, Carina, ed. *A Different Battle: Stories of Asian Pacific American Veterans.* Seattle: Wing Luke Asian Museum/University of Washington Press, 1999.

Densho Digital Archives. https://ddr.densho.org.

Densho Encyclopedia. https://encyclopedia.densho.org.

Franklin D. Roosevelt Presidential Library & Museum, Hyde Park, New York.

Higashide, Seiichi. *Adios to Tears: The Memoirs of a Japanese-Peruvian Internee in U.S. Concentration Camps.* Honolulu, HI: E & E Kudo, 1993.

Hong, Terry. "Michiko Nishiura Weglyn: (1926–) Costume designer, writer, activist." In *Notable Asian Americans*, ed. Helen Zia and Susan B. Gall. Detroit: Gale Research, 1995.

Kapitanoff, Nancy, and Sharon Yamato. *Out of Infamy: Michi Nishiura Weglyn.* Written, produced and directed by Kapitanoff and Yamato. Los Angeles: Nancy Kapitanoff and Sharon Yamato, 2009. DVD.

Leo Baeck Institute. Center for Jewish History, New York.

McCarthy, Sheryl Y. "Exposed: America's World War II Concentration Camps." *Mount Holyoke Alumnae Quarterly*, Fall 1997.

Michi Weglyn Collection. Japanese American National Museum, Los Angeles.

Mochizuki, Ken. *Meet Me at Higo: An Enduring Story of a Japanese American Family.* Seattle: Wing Luke Museum of the Asian Pacific American Experience, 2011.

Mochizuki, Ken. *Minidoka Memoirs: The Untold Story from the Yoshito Fujii Files.* Lake Forest Park, WA: Third Place Press, 2017.

Morse, Arthur D. *While Six Million Died: A Chronicle of American Apathy.* New York: Hart Publishing Company, 1967/Abrams Press, an imprint of Abrams, New York..

Shapiro, Harriet. "Michi." In *Gnomes and Knots*, ed. Judith Putterman. New York, Harper & Row, 1978.

Stone, Tanya Lee. *Peace Is a Chain Reaction: How World War II Japanese Balloon Bombs Brought People of Two Nations Together.* Somerville, MA: Candlewick Press, 2022

Weglyn, Michi Nishiura. Introduction by James A. Michener. *Years of Infamy: The Untold Story of America's Concentration Camps*, rev. ed. Seattle: University of Washington Press, 1996.

Permission to use text by Michi Weglyn and photographs of Michi Weglyn granted by the Estate of Michi Nishiura Weglyn. Phil Tajitsu Nash, Literary Executor.

Picture Credits

4 Japanese American National Museum (Gift of Michi and Walter M. Weglyn, 89.37.3); **5** Japanese American National Museum (Gift of Michi and Walter M. Weglyn, 89.37.5); **7** Japanese American National Museum (Gift of Michi and Walter M. Weglyn, 94.170.5_1); **11** Photo attributed to Dorothea Lange. Photograph from U.S. War Relocation Authority. Courtesy of the Library of Congress.; **12** Photo attributed to Dorothea Lange. Photograph from the Department of the Interior, War Relocation Authority. Courtesy of the National Archives.; **13** Photo attributed to Dorothea Lange. Photograph from the Department of the Interior, War Relocation Authority. Courtesy of the National Archives.; **17** Japanese American National Museum (Gift of Michi and Walter M. Weglyn, 94.170.11); **18** Japanese American National Museum (Gift of Michi Nishiura Weglyn 96.16.11_1); **19** Japanese American National Museum (Gift of Michi and Walter M. Weglyn, 94.170.24); **20** Japanese American National Museum (Gift of Michi Nishiura Weglyn 96.16.7); **22** Photograph from the Department of the Interior, War Relocation Authority. Courtesy of the National Archives.; **23** Japanese American National Museum (Gift of Michi and Walter M. Weglyn, 94.170.7); **26** Japanese American National Museum (Gift of Michi and Walter M. Weglyn, 94.170.6); **27** Japanese American National Museum (Gift of Michi and Walter M. Weglyn, 94.170.18); **28** Japanese American National Museum (Gift of in Memory of Hugo W. Wolter); **31** Japanese American National Museum (Gift of Michi Nishiura Weglyn 96.16.9); **33** Japanese American National Museum (Gift of Michi Nishiura Weglyn 96.16.8); **37** Photograph from the Department of Defense. Courtesy of the National Archives.; **39** Japanese American National Museum (Gift of Michi and Walter M. Weglyn, 94.170.17); **43** Japanese American National Museum (Gift of Edward G. and Blanche S. Chester/Gift of the Estate of Michi Weglyn 2000.77.78); **45** Frank Chin papers, Wyles Mss 103. Department of Special Research Collections, UC Santa Barbara Library, University of California, Santa Barbara.; **46** Frank Chin papers, Wyles Mss 103. Department of Special Research Collections, UC Santa Barbara Library, University of California, Santa Barbara.; **51** Japanese American National Museum (Gift of the Estate of Michi Weglyn 2000.77); **53** Japanese American National Museum (Gift of the Estate of Michi Weglyn 2000.77); **54** Japanese American National Museum (Gift of the Estate of Michi Weglyn 2000.77); **74** Courtesy of Pacific Citizen (www.pacificcitizen.org); **78** Courtesy of the Library of Congress; **81** Courtesy of the National Archives; **88–89** Courtesy of the Densho Digital Repository, the Ikeda Family Collection; **95** Japanese American National Museum (Gift of Michi Weglyn 96.33.2); **97** Courtesy of the Tule Lake Committee.; **99** From San Francisco Chronicle. © 1949 Hearst Newspapers. All rights reserved.; Used under license.; **108** Reproduced with permission of the University of Washington Press.; **111** Courtesy of the Ronald Reagan Presidential Library, National Archives and Records Administration; **119** Photo courtesy of the Wyoming Tribune Eagle; **120** Japanese American National Museum (Gift of the Estate of Michi Weglyn 2000.77); **123** Japanese American National Museum (Gift of the Estate of Michi Weglyn 2000.77); **125** Photo by Lia Chang. Japanese American National Museum (Gift of the Estate of Michi Weglyn 2000.77.3_4); **127** Japanese American National Museum (Gift of the Estate of Michi Weglyn 2000.77)

Page numbers in *italics* refer to illustrations.